ACUMEN™
PUBLISHING

ASIA LEADERSHIP™
TREK

ASIA LEADERSHIP™
INSTITUTE

Almaty, Ankara, Ashgabat, Astana, Baku, Bangkok, Beijing, Bishkek, Boston, Chisinau,
Colombo, Dhaka, Dushanbe, Hanoi, Ho Chi Minh City, Hong Kong, Jakarta, Kathmandu,
Kuala Lumpur, Kyiv, Manila, New Delhi, Phnom Penh, Seoul, Singapore, Taipei, Tashkent,
Thimphu, Tbilisi, Tokyo, Ulaanbaatar, Vientiane, Yangon

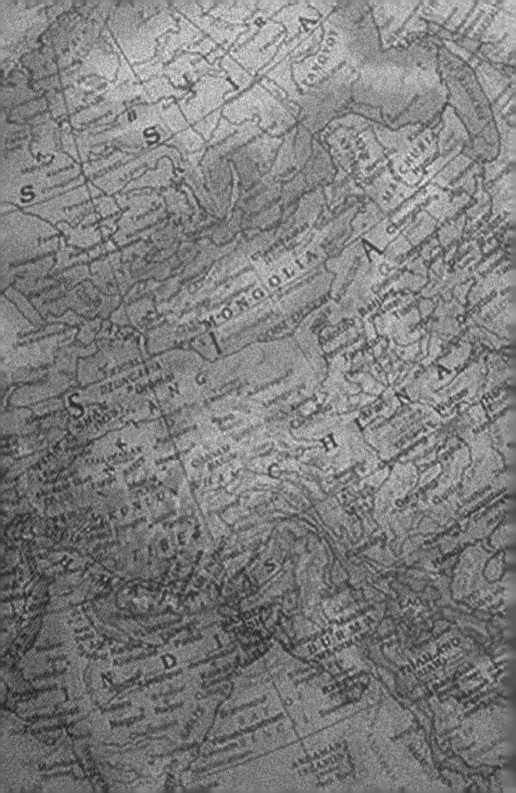

WE ARE
COMMITTED TO
FOSTERING
A DYNAMIC
AND THRIVING ASIA
WITH
CHANGE MAKERS
ENGAGED IN
RESPONSIBLE
AND EFFECTIVE
LEADERSHIP

RETHINKING
ASIA

Women's Leadership Retold

Rethinking Asia 8
Women's Leadership Retold

July 10, 2022
Copyright © 2022 by Center for Asia Leadership Initiatives

Printed in Seoul, Korea
A Publication of the Center for Asia Leadership Initiatives
Acumen Publishing
125 Cambridgepark Drive, Suite 301, Cambridge MA 02140, USA

Center for Asia Leadership Initiatives
Website: asialeadership.org, alf.asialeadership.org, online.asialeadership.org
Facebook: facebook.com/centerforasialeadership
Instagram/Twitter: @AsiaLeadership
LinkedIn: linkedin.com/company/center-for-asia-leadership-initiatives/
Weibo: @Asia_Trek

Library of Congress Control Number 2020942676

ISBN 978-0-9980917-0-9
US $14.99

For inquiries on partnership or sponsorship, or purchase of the publication, please email us at: cali@asialeadership.org

Disclaimer: This book is designed to provide information and motivation to our readers. It is sold with the understanding that the publisher is not engaged to render any type of psychological, legal, or any other kind of professional advice. The content of each article is the sole expression and opinion of its author, and not necessarily that of the publisher. No warranties or guarantees are expressed or implied by the publisher's choice to include any of the content in this volume. Neither the publisher nor the individual author(s) shall be liable for any physical, psychological, emotional, financial, or commercial damages, including, but not limited to, special, incidental, consequential or other damages. Our views and rights are the same: You are responsible for your own choices, actions, and results.

Cover design and typesetting courtesy of Luqman Hakim

Women's Leadership Retold
What to Keep, What to Leave Behind,
and What to Build

RETHINKING ASIA

8

edited by Hungsoo S. Kim

ACUMEN°
PUBLISHING

Let's shape our future to be
more humane and promising.

[signature]

The world needs more women leaders!
Not for the sake of equality—but
because on merit—women are eminently
capable, with unique skills that
will afford us all a brighter future!

Justin R. Hartley

The future is in your hands.
Make your noble dreams come true.

[signature]

May the words in these
pages meet you exactly
where you are, and
remind you that you
already have everything
you need to soar and
THRIVE!

[signature]

One of our greatest strengths is
our connection with one another

Rebecca Strand Stasel

This is a Kaleidoscope of
stories, experiences & learnings
It will inspire you, &
make you a part of authors'
lives. *[signature]*.

You are so much more than
you think you are. Believe.

[signature]

Be inspired
and inspire

Mieke

Shine bright into this
world. Have the courage
to leave your mark.

Daria Istrate

*To all the aspiring women and men
leaders of this world*

| Table of Contents |

•••

Part 2 • Developing Inner Capacities: 7 Leadership Lessons that Women Can Learn from Women

Part 3 • Forging the Allyship: 2 Leadership Lessons that Everyone Can Learn from Men

Part 4 • The Epilogue

I About the Editor I

•••

Hungsoo S. Kim, a Korean national, is the Founding President of the Center for Asia Leadership. Passionate about nurturing and empowering talent in Asia, he runs over 50 projects and programs annually to help decision-makers and emerging leaders think deeply and broadly about their responsibilities and their ability to help their respective communities and organizations thrive. Organizational Adaptability, Legacy Management, Strategic Foresight, ESG, Trust-building, Ethics, and Power & Influence are among the key areas of his research, teaching, coaching, and consulting.

To date, some 52,000 leaders, representing 400 organizations from the international, governmental, political, corporate and non-profit spheres, in 83 cities and 31 countries in Asia, have benefitted from his work. He has also organized numerous international conferences in which over 350 global leaders, along with 4,000 in-person attendants and over 100,000 online participants annually have joined forces to discuss possible solutions for the pressing issues currently confronting Asia and the world. Han Duck-soo, Mahathir Mohamad, Scott Morrison, Barack Obama, David Cameron, and Michelle Obama, are among the speakers invited in the past.

Prior to establishing the Center, Hungsoo worked for 15 years in a wide range of sectors, from strategy consulting, non-profits, and social entrepreneurship to international development, politics, the military, and government work. The UN, UNESCO, Samsung, SK, and Petronas are among the organizations he had worked with or for. However, he takes deepest pride in having run one of Korea's first social enterprises, which provided economic opportunities to 350 underserved families.

Hungsoo has served as a visiting fellow at the Asia Center at Harvard University and the Kellogg School of Management in Northwestern University. He holds an MPA from Harvard, an MA from Seoul National, and an LLB from Handong Universities. He is the editor of 14 books and regularly writes opinion pieces and editorials. His publications cover a wide range of genres, from policy proposals and evaluations to travelogues and academic pieces on political reform, innovation, education, entrepreneurship, economic development, education, the future of work, and women's leadership.

I About the Contributors I

•••

Justin Hartley is the Founder and CEO of Model Leadership, a company designed to help individuals maximize and realize their potential: through good character & self-leadership; mental mastery; and outstanding communication & influence.

His achievements include co-founding Australia's first non-profit for children suffering from chronic pain; working for Samaritans (Central London) in supporting people who were actively suicidal; serving as a full-time primary caregiver for his mother, who suffered from Alzheimer's disease; and working in the media as a memory and mental health expert. He is also a former Guinness World Record Holder in memory; an Australian Memory Champion; and a representative for his country in memory and mental-calculation world championships.

Justin holds several degrees from the University of Queensland, including first-class honors in Economics and Finance; an MPA from Harvard, where he was a Fulbright Scholar and Kennedy Fellow; and an MSc from the University of Oxford. A coach, speaker, trainer, scholar, and author, Justin has worked with leaders around the world, including Prime Ministers, Presidents, and Executives. He is passionate about mentoring and coaching aspiring and emerging leaders.

Daria Istrate is a Lecturer at the Harvard Business School and has an extensive background in strategy: she routinely advises companies on cross-border acquisitions, mergers, and restructuring in healthcare, energy, and logistics. Over the past ten years, she has honed her expertise in the development and commercialization of life-changing cancer treatments and is currently working with Genentech, based in San Francisco. She has also founded a private educational institution in her home country of Romania and is actively working on growing education investments in Eastern Europe.

Daria is a champion of public-private partnerships and has worked with the World Health Organization and the World Food Program to support technology with investments, with the aim of improving health and education in Sub-Saharan Africa. She has lived and worked on three continents and holds an MBA from Harvard University. She is also a contributing member of the Innovation and Entrepreneurship Program at Stanford University. An angel investor in several ventures in healthcare and logistics, she is interested in partnering with visionary entrepreneurial minds to bring innovative technologies to market.

Nikita Jain is the CEO and Founder of Eubrics.com and an engineer with a Master's degree in Human Resources. She has accrued a decade of consulting experience with such global organizations as PwC, Korn Ferry, and EY. Nikita is also a certified coach and assessor who has worked with over 100 enterprises and over 1,000 individuals on their leadership journeys. She is an active author for national-level research papers. Before starting Eubrics.com, an AI platform for behavioral change, Nikita built several million-dollar businesses and technology platforms to improve the skills and employability of the global workforce.

Shahzad Khan is a Silicon Valley entrepreneur, international business leader, and investor and advisor for early-stage technology companies. With two decades of experience in driving strategy, innovation, and organizational change, Shahzad has spent his career leading transformational growth for organizations spanning continents and industries.

In his early career Shahzad worked as a technologist at Accenture. He then established and managed his own international consulting practice, where he worked with organizations including AT&T, Verizon, Nortel, and Cisco Systems. Subsequently, Shahzad co-founded a digital marketing company headquartered in Ukraine, which pioneers analytics to drive marketing effectiveness across platforms for an array of global clients. For the past five years, Shahzad has brought his leadership to the healthcare space, providing strategic insights for Gilead Sciences and Roche. Consistent throughout his career is Shahzad's passion for leveraging data to guide strategy and inspiring individuals to execute transformational change.

Shahzad holds a B.S. in Economics and Computer Science and an M.S. in Industrial Engineering and Operations Research from UC Berkeley, and is currently furthering his executive education at Stanford's Graduate School of Business.

Mieke Klanker is a consultant in finance passionate about creating change in the corporate world. Having worked over ten years in mergers and acquisitions across Europe, Asia, the Middle East, and the Americas, her current focus is on embedding sustainability and ESG in finance and decision making. Her innate curiosity and desire to learn from and experience other cultures has brought her to study, work and live in over 10 countries and to speak over 5 languages. Mieke is a diversity and inclusion advocate, having served as board member of Lean In Netherlands, a foundation supporting women to achieve their ambitions and work towards creating an equal world.

Mieke holds a Bachelor's degree in Anthropology from the Vrije Universiteit Amsterdam and obtained a Master's degree in International Political Economy from Sciences Po Paris. Hailing from the Netherlands, she enjoys spending her time off in the mountains.

Jane Jiyoung Park is a pianist, an entrepreneur, and the mother of three beautiful children. Her passion for music was manifest when she started playing piano at the age of four; she subsequently won the All Paris, All France, and All Europe competitions starting at the age of ten. Due to her father's profession as a journalist, she lived in three continents while growing up. She speaks Korean, French, and English, with a working knowledge of Spanish.

After five years spent teaching English, she co-led SBT F&B, Inc., as Executive Director. This company was one of Korea's first social enterprises, comprising three companies and providing economic opportunities to 350 low-income families. She also spearheaded Impact Korea, a non-profit that ran leadership capacity-building and community-service programs for 400 young people in Korea. In addition, she co-led a choir of 120 children. Her passion is to help other individuals discover life's purpose and thrive.

Rebecca Stroud Stasel is a certified K-12 teacher and a researcher of comparative and international education and of educational policy and leadership. She completed her Ph.D. at Queen's University in Canada. Her research interests also include drama education, arts-based methodologies, and Indigenous epistemologies. Her K-12 teaching career spans 20 years and 5 countries. Her doctoral studies took her to Southeast and East Asia to explore educator acculturation, along with 17 other "sojourning" teachers and educational leaders. Her findings revealed common policy-scapes, self-leadership, and leadership strategies to support acculturation, an effective onboarding and induction program, the effect of the pandemic upon sojourning educators and leaders, and the basis for an educator acculturation framework. Rebecca writes poetry and short works of fiction, and she enjoys spending time outdoors and traveling.

Carrie Tan also known as CoachCarrie is a transformative healer, coach and member of Parliament in Singapore. She founded Daughters Of Tomorrow, a women's charity, followed by Rise Community, a men's charity, to lift up those who have the least. "Lightbearers" at www.lbinc.co is her coaching practice, to heal the wounds of humanity through teaching and guiding those seeking truth and the light within. Her articles are available on LiveMore, a free personal development app bringing learning and community to wellness seekers.

Ami Valdemoro is a leadership coach, health advocate, and entrepreneur, with fifteen years of experience in leading and managing impact investments around the world. Among other achievements, she ran the Africa Tobacco Control Consortium, funded by the Bill & Melinda Gates Foundation; as Executive Director, she set up the social-impact portfolio of the first U.S.-registered Benefit corporation in the Philippines, Generation HOPE; and she now sits on the Board of Liter of Light, a community-based solar-lighting initiative that annually gives power to over one million beneficiaries around the world.

Through her company Three Points Ventures, Ami has trained thousands of professionals across Asia in leadership, communication, and growth. Ami helps purpose-driven leaders design creative strategies to reach their goals with balance and ease. By listening, asking questions, and sharing key insights, she helps her clients come up with ways that they might act, think, or be different, so that they can start and lead enterprises with a lasting impact.

Ami is a core member of the teaching faculty at the Center for Asia Leadership, with whom she has published works on teaching and practicing leadership in the region. She received her Master's degree from the Harvard Kennedy School and her Bachelor's degree, with honors, from Georgetown University.

| Foreword |

●●●

For the past forty years, as a policy-maker, an academician, a diplomat, a social activist, and an author, I have committed my life to helping communities and individuals from various backgrounds develop a strong commitment to advancing public interests, by thinking deeply and broadly about our responsibilities to our communities and by acting strategically to generate positive outcomes. It is my humble opinion that each one of us is on a life-long leadership journey that requires continuous learning—learning that will help us hone and harness our ability to lead and that, when added to the efforts of others, will dramatically improve our world's conditions.

Humans have been on this journey for centuries: even ancient thinkers like Confucius, Plato, and Machiavelli maintained that learning to lead was the work of a lifetime. Yet too often, today, we see contemporary leaders pursuing windfalls or low-hanging fruit, entrenched in the belief that learning to lead can be accomplished quickly and easily, in a matter of few days or weeks, sometimes simply by getting hold of a certificate that may or may not have any value.

Since 2012, Mr. Hungsoo Kim, the editor of this volume, and I have worked together in many different capacities, including organizing public events, running leadership programs, and executing public diplomacy projects throughout Asia. Thanks to these varied efforts, I have had a chance to witness Hungsoo's purposeful work and to learn in depth about what he aspires to accomplish through the Center for Asia Leadership Initiatives (CALI), a social-profit organization that he established when he was still a student at Harvard.

Among the many things he has shared with me, one point instantly caught my attention and has stayed with me ever since: namely, his effort to help leaders mobilize their key stakeholders to embrace change and make critical adaptations that will define their fate by ensuring survival and growth. In line with this effort, he has also made a conscious and genuine endeavor to continually enhance his various programs and projects—the teaching, consulting, coaching, conferences, and publications all sponsored by CALI, so that they can nurture and support real leaders who will improve our circumstances both in Asia and all over the world.

I sincerely hope that Hungsoo's efforts will challenge and redefine the practice of leadership in our current times. And I consider this book deeply important to that effort: within these pages, Hungsoo and his co-authors focus on the very important topic of gender bias and discrimination, especially from the standpoint of women—single and married, working and non-working, Asian and Western. The authors explore the array of challenges that professional women and female leaders too often encounter, including behavioral and cultural barriers arising from systemic constraints, persistent stereotypes, and historically uneven playing fields.

The book is even more essential because of the authors' candid sharing of many valuable ideas, practices, frameworks, and methodologies, which speak to both women and men on how the many obstacles and gaps faced by women can be combated and corrected. I found these insights, coupled with the authors' personal stories and firsthand examples, highly practical and relevant, as they were based on the authors' own experiences, observations, and research. Together the chapters encompass several different spheres of modern leadership, from government and politics to businesses and communities. While they are mainly aimed toward readers in Asia, a place where women face some of the most difficult challenges in the world, individuals in all countries of the world will find much to value in this volume.

As someone who has chaired a nonprofit championing women's rights, as well as supporting the children of multicultural families, individuals with disabilities, and neglected international orphans of Korean descent, I hold the subject of women's leadership dear to my heart. I firmly believe that the obstacles confronting women should be addressed not merely for the sake of diversity and inclusion but because women are just as capable and gifted as men—if not more so in certain areas.

An article published in *The Guardian* in June 2022 made me wonder how my country of Korea might pioneer the fight for the "underrepresented sex" in Asia. According to the article, "The EU has agreed that companies will face mandatory quotas to ensure women have at least 40% of seats on corporate boards." Some people in Asia might debate the effectiveness of this approach, but I believe that a similar method could help us become more inclusive and equitable in Asia as well.

As the Foreign Minister of Korea, I have had the privilege of witnessing several of my counterparts trailblazing for their fellow women, including Ursula von der Leyen, President of the European Commission; Christine Lagarde, President of the European Central Bank; Ngozi Okonjo-Iweala, Director General of the World Trade Organization; Olha Stefanishyna, Ukrainian Deputy Prime Minister; and many more.

Hungsoo recently told me that he has been working to compile and publish this book of essays since 2016. Thanks to its complex nature, however, it didn't come to life until now, serving as the eighth volume of the ten-volume *Rethinking Asia* series. I commend him highly for persisting in his initiative and not giving up on his decision to publish the book.

As a member of CALI's Global Advisory Council, I have witnessed how the *Rethinking Asia* series has evolved. Its first five volumes are collections of insights and lessons drawn from the Asia Leadership Trek, a biannual study and public-service tour that Hungsoo and his colleagues organize; since 2012, they have reached eighty-three cities in thirty-one countries. This volume is the third in the next set of five, which together present CALI's well-grounded, research-backed recommendations for leadership policy and strategy. Topics explored earlier in the series include the Future of Work, Sustainability, Governance, and Innovation, among others.

It gives me profound joy to know that this book will aid many readers as they continue their journeys as leaders, both within and beyond their own communities, helping to liberate the world from the forces that are threatening to pull us apart. The book gives me hope that all of the people involved in CALI's initiatives—faculty, students, and readers alike—will contribute in bringing about better living conditions for the many peoples of Asia.

Enjoy the journey!

Dr. Park Jin
D.Phil, Oxford University
MPA, Harvard University
Minister of Foreign Affairs, Republic of Korea

Introduction

The Triggers & Journey Behind This Book

Hungsoo S. Kim
Harvard MPA
Founding President, Center for Asia Leadership

●●●

The period from 2014 to 2019 was one of the most exhilarating times of my life. As an organizer of the Asia Leadership Treks, a series of study tours and community-service programs that took place throughout Asia, I traveled with a total of about 500 Harvard scholars and graduate students to 83 cities in 31 countries, meeting and learning from key figures and decision-makers in the spheres of government, politics, business, and grassroots enterprises, while also sharing our own knowledge and skills with the region's emerging leaders. This first-hand exposure involved roundtables, conferences, networking events, and site visits, and gave us an array of unique, beyond-the-classroom learning experiences.

One of the key highlights for me during these Treks was learning about the remarkable achievements of women leaders from all walks of life. A Nobel Laureate, a human-rights activist in Kathmandu, a Senior Economic Advisor to the Turkish President, the first female

Chief Justice of the Philippine Supreme Court, the Governor of the Malaysian Central Bank—from all of these women and more, we learned how, as leaders, they have helped their respective communities to confront challenges and improve people's lives and livelihoods.

Alongside the Treks, I spearheaded numerous capacity-building programs in the region, and in all of these programs I was struck by the high participation of women in our conferences, seminars, and master-classes. Engaging in conversations with these women led me to recognize a critical blind spot in my own knowledge: I had a limited understanding of the systemic constraints on women, constraints that often make it difficult for them to achieve their personal and professional aspirations and to gain and maintain positions of authority. Women more than men, due to external circumstances, face persistent difficulties in reaching positions of influence. Earlier in my life I didn't understand this situation well from a woman's standpoint, but with the exposure I have gained through the Treks and the programs I run, I have learned a great deal about the cultural, religious, economic, political, and social factors that historically—and still today in many places—have pushed women into subordinate positions. Today these constraints are more prominent in Asia than in the West, but examples can be found all too frequently all over the world.

To use an instance from own experience: my wife is a pianist, and toward the end of my studies at Harvard, she planned to pursue her work in composition and performance at one of the world's most renowned contemporary music schools, based in Boston. However, though she gained admission to the school thanks to her talent and ambition, the constraints of our life together interfered with her plans. As the mother of three small children and the wife of a man who would soon relocate to Asia, her options were limited, and she was forced to let go of the opportunity.

There are countless similar examples of women facing gender-specific constraints, in all shapes and forms, on a daily basis throughout the world. Women's starting lines, all too often, lie far behind those of the men. Of course, we also hear stories of successful women like Ursula von der Leyen, the President of the European Commission, who rose through the ranks to her current leadership position even as a mother of seven,[1] and many others, including the heads of YouTube, Oracle, General Motors, AMD, and IBM.[2] Given the challenges that they and so many other women face, I have grown more and more interested in how they were able to fight and rise up, gaining both formal and informal authorities.

Such success stories, as I have said, are more possible in the West—despite many hurdles that still remain there—than in the East, as illustrated by the fact that the above-mentioned figures are all from the Western world. This disparity is the first broad area that this book will explore: the nature of the systemic constraints faced by women in the East and in the West, and the similarities and differences between them. Through this comparison, the book aims to offer insight into the reasons underlying the ample leadership opportunities available to women in the West, and the ways in which women in the East can gain greater freedom and authorities to lead. We seek to offer in this book a wide-ranging and balanced perspective on these questions.

My own work, which focuses on helping women and men in Asia through Harvard-inspired frameworks and practices of teaching, coaching, and consulting, aims to develop leadership qualities that will make every participant an influential leader in his or her own field. From my recent experiences, I know that such work requires a

1   www.theguardian.com/world/2019/jul/02/women-to-head-top-eu-institutions-for -first-time.
2   www.theceomagazine.com/business/management-leadership/female-ceos/.

carefully designed approach, especially for women. Developing individual leadership attributes is indeed important for women as they strive to achieve their personal goals, but for our work to achieve its intended purpose of helping many people become leaders in all realms, it must take into account the special challenges that women face. Thus, the second area that this book will explore is how people within both Eastern and Western communities discuss the concept of leadership, and which qualities they deem most important for women who aim to become leaders.

Over the years of my educative journey, I have felt a strong desire to document what I and my colleagues have seen and heard—the stories, insights, and lessons we've gained. This book is the eighth in our ten-volume series Rethinking Asia. I am proud to say that the Center has published one book every year since 2015, covering a wide range of topics pertinent to today's Asia. The theme of this book, women's leadership, is especially timely for 2022, which is colored with greater uncertainties, disruptions, hostilities, and divisions than any of us are used to, and which calls for us as both leaders and citizens of the world to create more inclusive and sustainable communities, and to diminish the deepening fault-lines of race, ethnicity, gender, politics, and values.

Personally, I believe that a leadership is a choice—a good-willed activity that engages with the present in the hope of a better tomorrow. The power to exercise leadership comes from within and aims to bring about improvements in our lives and the conditions around us. That said, though women are, of course, as capable and strong-willed as men, for women's leadership to flourish in a broader, societal context, it can't be just the women alone exerting themselves. Achieving a true equality of leadership across the world requires an active partnership between men and women, in which both groups join forces to learn about the blind-spots and pain-points that women encounter. Once these constraints are recognized, both men and women must work to mitigate—if not eliminate—them, and also to emphasize and improve the positive elements of our communities. In sum, to overcome systemic obstacles to gender equality, improve women's lives, and increase their opportunities for advancement, both women and men must exercise effective leadership; this is the last area that this book will delve into.

Focusing on the three areas mentioned above, the book offers stories and lessons from ten contributors who are both women and men, coming from varying communities across the globe and a range of professional backgrounds. These contributors provide plenty of food for thought and vigorous calls to action in the fight for a better tomorrow. The book is designed for both women and men, but we hope that it will be particularly inspiring for women. The stories it contains demonstrate how individuals can think and act courageously by recognizing and building their own capacities, gaining credibility, and winning allies to create a world that is closer to what they envision.

In addition, all of the contributors in this book argue that leadership is an everyday quality: there are and will always be challenges for everyone and opportunities for everyone to lead. Whether or not we confront these challenges and embrace these opportunities is for each of us to decide—a choice that every person makes. If we want to achieve our aspirations, we must choose to engage with a complex and challenging world.

Before we set sail, let me thank a few people who made this publication possible. First and foremost, I thank the contributors, who spared some of their precious time to document valuable stories from their lives; without their efforts, the lessons in these pages could not have reached our readers. I also extend deep gratitude to my team at the Center for Asia Leadership Initiatives, whose insights have added

great value to this book.
   Enjoy reading, everyone!

Hungsoo S. Kim
Founding President, CALI

Part 1

:

The Perspective

| Chapter 01 |
Defining this Book's Purpose

Hungsoo S. Kim
Harvard MPA
Founding President, Center for Asia Leadership

● ● ●

The Approach

In her study of the political culture in Asia, Andrea Fleschenberg observes a "paradoxical phenomenon":[1] on the one hand, Asia contains a large number of patriarchal and paternalistic socio-cultural and political structures, which posit that men are better equipped than women to exercise power in the public domain;[2] on the other hand, many Asian women hold positions as head of state, most notably in South and Southeast Asia. With the rise of these "Asian tigresses," a relatively large body of research has emerged to explain this phenomenon.

---

1   Fleschenberg, Andrea, et al., Handbuch Spitzenpolitikerinnen, 2008, p. 26.
2   Patriarchal Power As A Conceptual Tool For Gender History.
    www.tandfonline.com/doi/full/10.1080/13642529.2022.2037864.

The prominence of Asia's "dynastic political culture"—the majority of the female heads of state are either daughters or widows of popular male nationalist politicians—is the most influential explanation.[3] Yet, while the dynastic factor certainly offers one method of understanding the rise of the female political leader, I believe that overstating the symbolic powers of the deceased or exiled male leaders does more harm than good, as it reinforces the claim that family background and affiliation are the core factors contributing to the women's rise, thus downplaying the strengths, talents, and potential of the women themselves. It also undermines the efforts of other women who, without any influential family affiliations, are still able to launch and sustain successful careers.

Citing Mao Zedong's statement that "women hold up half the sky," this book discusses women as equal contributors to the growth of society, not just within the political realm—though political issues figure prominently—but also in the economic, social, and cultural realms.

As I mentioned in my Introduction, the idea for creating a book on this topic originated in the Treks I have led since 2014. Trek participants, mainly Harvard scholars and students, have had the honor of meeting many inspirational women leaders, who described their inspiring life journeys and explained how they successfully overcame many socioeconomic, political, and cultural barriers to take on the mantle of leadership.

There remains a clear lack of awareness in both the East and the West of positive female role models in leadership positions. Exposure to a diverse range of women leaders, including those who contributed to this book, will be crucial in helping today's young women learn what roles they may play in order to become effective agents of change in their communities, and in helping today's young men

---

3   Amirell, Stefan E. www.tandfonline.com/doi/abs/12259276.2012.11666126.

understand that women are just as inherently capable of becoming effective leaders as they are themselves. This book deliberately moves away from popular debates on the dynastic elements to focus instead on women leaders themselves—the social contexts in which they were brought up and now seek to change, their stories of challenges and successes, and their leadership styles and actions for achieving positive change in their communities. It also looks into effective male allyship models: the various approaches that men can take to help advance women's stature and success.

By presenting detailed analyses as well as intimate first-hand accounts from these contributors, who have succeeded in breaking away from traditional expectations and societal norms to take on meaningful leadership roles in various roles and capacities, this book seeks to empower, motivate, and send a message of hope and inspiration to all aspiring female and male leaders in Asia and the world.

The Audience

To my knowledge, few publications offer a comparative analysis of the leadership journeys, challenges, approaches, and triumphs of female leaders from both the West and the East.

The West has seen many efforts to create a more equitable society, despite a host of systemic challenges. With America's new administration in place, championing these endeavors, and with the ever-growing presence of women in the West as leaders and top decision-makers in all domains of society, we have great hopes of seeing ever more Western women taking on leadership roles in the future.

In Asia, the world's dominant economic powerhouse,[4] women face greater barriers. As defined by the United Nations, Asia is composed of 48 nations and is home to two-thirds of the global population,[5] including two billion women.[6] Many of its leaders, both women and men, have achieved milestone accomplishments in addressing important societal issues. However, we still have a long way to go. Rampant corruption, malfunctioning governance systems, a growing digital and knowledge divide, and a widening income gap—as well as a persistently deep and wide gender gap—are still prevalent in many parts of Asia.

As I said in the Introduction, solving all of these challenges requires the work of both women and men: we must join forces to confront the problems surrounding us, and men, in particular, need to recognize women's capacity for leadership, acknowledge and resist their own biases, stop oppressing women, and fight actively for women's rights. Women, on the other hand, must fight back against systemic barriers, show up and speak up on the many problems hampering their social progress, and work to achieve systemic changes so that our social, economic, and cultural systems no longer favor men.

In Asia today, more women than ever before have access to tertiary education,[7] which gives them far greater opportunities within the labor market. In fact, in several Asian countries women form more than half the labor force,[8] with a growing number of women holding positions of high authority. This trend needs to continue to accelerate—and this can happen only when both women and men embrace this effort.

By sharing the stories of the contributors featured here, this volume will both fill a gap in current leadership books and provide a powerful source of inspiration for women—and men—in Asia and beyond.

---

4   www.weforum.org/agenda/2019/07/the-dawn-of-the-asian-century/.
5   www.un.org/en/global-issues/population.
6   www.asia.nikkei.com/Spotlight/The-Big-Story/The-new-population-bomb.
7   www.indiatoday.in/education-today/featurephilia/story/more-women-are-pursuing-higher-education-now-than-ever-before-1921750-2022-03-08.
8   www.urmati-20-ani-crestere-economica-romania-inregistrat-cea-mare-crestere-economica-un

Their stories provide an illuminating window into today's world, not only informing readers of the many different political frameworks and economic policies operating in the West and the East, but also demonstrating the innovative power and striking personalities of leaders in both regions. Overall, I hope that this book will give readers from both worlds insightful glimpses into an effective ethos of leadership, through the perspectives of ten accomplished and well-respected leaders.

The Criteria

We wanted to ensure that openness, authenticity, practicality, relatability, and inspiration were in place in each chapter in this book, so that readers could both connect to the contributing authors and walk away with a clear plan of action. As a result, each chapter has been written with four fundamental elements embedded in it:

1. *Challenges/Contexts:* stories of personal challenge(s) in facing systemic hurdles borne of cultural, religious, social, economic, and/or political circumstances.

2. *Enablers:* stories showing how enablers came to the authors' aid in overcoming their challenges and achieving their aspirations. This help might be (a) personal, fostering the authors' interests, personality, upbringing, experiences, exposures, or influences; (b) relational, in the form of key influencers, partners, or thought-provokers, and/or (c) professional, supporting the authors' studies, activities, expertise, experiences, and goals.

3. *Legitimacy:* work done by the authors that illustrates good intentions and positive impacts, as evinced by wider support from their communities. Such work might also be illustrated by their values or credos, which permeate their personal and professional lives and

have helped them reach their current standing today.

4. *Lessons:* messages that serve not to advance the authors' personal interests but to help our readers grasp key leadership concepts and actionable insights, offering practical calls to action for both women and men.

The Structure

This book is divided into two parts. The first contains chapters by women primarily addressing their fellow women, while the second section offers chapters by men addressing both women and men. By sharing personal stories and accounts of challenges they have overcome, our authors provide valuable lessons and calls to action that encapsulate their key messages and encourage immediate application by our readers.

Overall, the book contains many valuable gems that we gleaned from multiple rounds of discussions and review. I hope that what you find in these pages will inspire you deeply and prompt you to take part in advancing our cause of creating a more promising, hopeful, and equitable global community. Now let the journey begin!

Part 2

. . .

Developing Inner Capacities

| Chapter 02 |

Either/Or, Or Both?

How Accepting and Integrating Assertive and Empathetic Approaches Creates Better Leadership

Ami Valdemoro
Harvard MPP
CEO, Three Points Ventures

● ● ●

So Tell Me, What Exactly Is Women's Leadership Anyway?

I'm sitting on one side of a computer screen, perplexed at the gentleman who's just asked me to define women's leadership. Full stop.

There is silence on both ends of the call, but believe me, my inner monologue is epically loud. On the one hand, I'm flattered that this person has reached out to me based on my perceived expertise. He clearly feels I have a unique perspective, one he can trust. My ego, which craves validation, relishes the fact that he sees me as an authority on this subject and believes I have something genuine and authentic to say.

On the other hand, I can't help but figuratively smack my head in disbelief. Why are we even having this conversation? Why does women's leadership still have to be defined as different from men's leadership? Why do women always have to do the work to educate men about what women's issues are—not just with leadership, but with other things too?

The silence seems to last forever while I wage this ancient battle in my head. I can only imagine what my client is seeing on the other end of our Zoom call.

The devil's advocate wins, this time. I take a breath and turn the question back to him: "What do you think? Is women's leadership really any different from just plain old leadership? Or do you only think it has to be different?"

In the Beginning

When I was growing up, it was just my parents, my older sister, and me. Other than the fact that my dad insisted we always have a male dog as an ally for him in a house full of females, I always felt I could do anything that boys could. I played sports, got dirty, and never felt constrained by being a girl in the way my parents treated or raised me. The only requirement that I ever felt—and it was always present—was to put my best effort into whatever I was doing, and to walk in the world with dignity and integrity.

It was only when I got to school and encountered other cultures and contexts that I realized my experience was not universal.

I was the first person in my family to be born and raised in the U.S. My parents and sister were all born in the Philippines and emigrated to the U.S. before I came along. Our ties to the Philippines are still strong, so my entire existence has straddled two continents, America and Asia, each with its own perspective on the roles that women should play at home, at work, and in society.

In Filipino culture, women traditionally make the vast majority of economic decisions in the household, and this tradition is willingly accepted by most families. It was the first country in Asia to have a female President, an act that has been repeated since then. The Philippines consistently ranks at the top of all lists measuring gender parity and equality. In some ways, the country has moved beyond conversations on gender because women have succeeded in displaying leadership at every level.

I can see this achievement mirrored in my own family history, particularly in my grandmothers, Amada and Michaela, for whom I am named. Both of them were empowered women: one raised eleven children who all completed college and went on to lead successful, meaningful lives of purpose; and one earned a Ph.D., rising up to the top echelons of education as Dean of the Philippine Women's University. Their achievements helped me to grow up thinking and feeling that I could do anything.

As a child in the U.S., I learned the values of resourcefulness, determination, and a "can do" spirit. At its best, my upbringing in American culture encouraged me to pursue ambitious goals (and yes, be a bit competitive). At its worst, it reeked of arrogance, an assumption that because I could do something, I knew how to do it and could do it better than others.

Reflecting on my origins and foundations, I now see why a part of me was puzzled when the man on my Zoom call asked me to define "women's leadership." For my whole life, I've been in a position of access and privilege that has allowed me to remove gender from my view of the world, simply because there was nothing I thought I couldn't do, be, or say.

This is not the case in many parts of the world, including Asia, where women are still viewed as outliers or outsiders in leadership spaces, and countries with traditionally patriarchal structures, where women continue to be excluded from decision-making.

I by no means want to downplay the deep challenges that still exist for women striving to gain basic rights and equality around the world. I also do not want to discount the many other factors besides gender that color one's approach to leadership. For the purposes of this reflection piece, however, I will speak from my direct experience and focus on two different approaches to leadership that are often associated with gender, which I will call "assertive" and "empathetic."

The conversation with the gentleman on Zoom got me thinking. What was it that made my experience different, and how can we change conversations about "women's leadership" so that, rather than defining it as a category on its own, we can instead think and talk about "leadership" as a multi-faceted concept applicable to men and women alike?

Imported Using Local Parts

When I started my career, at a company in the U.S., people saw me as a diplomat—someone who was polite, soft-spoken, and always interested in doing things for the benefit of my team. When I first moved to the Philippines eight years ago, however, the perception of me could not have been more different. There, people viewed me as acting strong and assertive—in fact, too strong and too assertive.

I remember sitting in a meeting with branding consultants who were trying to help the startup I was advising to position themselves in their industry. At some point in our discussion, we were talking about spokespeople: who was best placed to represent the organization at conferences, functions, and client meetings. Someone volunteered my name, but one of the consultants in the room told me, "Malakas ang dating mo!" Or in English, "You don't come across as friendly or approachable!"

WHAT?! Seriously?

Once again, I had to catch my breath. I couldn't believe what I had just heard.

It's a tough pill to swallow, that people don't see you as approachable when you believe you are inviting openness and collaboration. What's more, the assertion that I came across as "malakas," or "strong," had negative implications in the Philippines. It was not viewed as a positive attribute to be direct and resolute and to know what I wanted (and didn't want).

Hearing the consultant's words felt like salt on an open wound. Not only was I unaware of how people perceived me; the way in which I was viewed—based on behaviors that I had grown up accepting and integrating into my management and leadership style—was "bad." I was the same person, but in two completely different contexts. There was a palpable imbalance in the way I approached the outside world and the way that approach was viewed, in terms of the effectiveness—or ineffectiveness—of my management and leadership skills.

Looking back now, I realize that I was struggling to integrate two parts of myself: the part that values assertiveness, directness, and action, which in many cultures are considered "masculine" traits; and the part that embraces intuition, empathy, and consensus, which in many cultures are considered "feminine" traits. In an unfamiliar place like Manila, where I had just moved, I defaulted to a more Western, go-getter, assertive approach, and as a result I ended up either alienating people or resentfully feeling forced into adopting a more empathetic, docile approach. Doing the latter felt like a betrayal of my training, education, and upbringing; I yearned to stand up and make my voice heard.

At the same time, I could not feel that I was operating with full integrity when I pushed aside the parts of me that did want to make decisions from a consensus-based, compassionate place. It was as if I were at war within myself.

For a long time after that experience, I laid the blame on others—it was their fault that they viewed me in a particular way. But this was an arrogant response, one made out of self-defense. It was only when I started working towards my Master's-level coaching certification that I understood: the key lay not in faulting others but in focusing on my own work to integrate the two parts of myself.

Either/Or, or Both?

Historically, effective leadership has been defined as being ambitious and assertive, valuing hustle, placing an emphasis on winning vs. losing, and nurturing a competitive spirit (which at its best can be healthy, but at its worst can be debilitating). Many of these traits have been traditionally associated with men. And in many situations, these traits have enabled clans, cultures, and countries to survive and thrive, defining what they stood for and allowing leaders to provide, in the Adaptive Leadership language of Ron Heifetz and Marty Linsky, "protection, direction, and order."[1] However, we've seen many recent examples of these assertive, "masculine" traits becoming limiting, or, when taken to their extremes, toxic. A "winner take all" mentality and the impulse to push forward with a total absence of understanding, let alone compassion, for others has led to division, populism, and regression.

At the same time, for as long as we have existed in social structures, a subcurrent has run alongside these "assertive" behaviors, a management style traditionally associated with women. For the purposes of this article, I will call this style "empathetic." It is an approach based on intuition, "soft power," networking, and com-

---

1   Heifetz, Ron and Marty Linsky, "Leadership on the Line: Staying Alive Through the Dangers of Leading." Harvard Business Review Press. Cambridge, MA: 2002.

passion, and is often connected with service or care-oriented professions. Historically, it was also assumed to be less effective. In some contexts, particularly in the corporate world, demonstrating care, vulnerability, and emotion at work is still deemed "unsuitable," especially if a woman exhibits these qualities. One need only look at media articles to see that the idea of women being "too emotional to lead" has governed most of corporate culture up until only recently.

In the past few years, however, as discussions around "toxic masculinity" have come to the forefront, along with manifestations like the #MeToo movement occurring around the world, many have tried to give more voice and space to this empathetic style of leadership, particularly in the West.

My struggle to integrate my own assertive and empathetic sides mirrors a larger challenge that we face of defining and practicing leadership. Too often, we think of "men's leadership" and "women's leadership" as two different, mutually exclusive concepts. But what if they're not different after all?

The truth is we each have both assertive and empathetic traits within us, and when we favor one over the other consistently, we are not in balance. So what if, instead of speaking in "either/or" statements and valuing one approach over another, we think instead about integration and adopt the belief that both leadership styles can be effective, and that we all have the tendency toward both styles within us?

I realize that this may be an uncomfortable notion, since it goes against the norms and traditions of many cultures, as Edgar Ramirez pointed out in the quote that closes this chapter. But viewing leadership as a multi-faceted concept accessible to all can be beneficial to both men and women. Why? For women leaders, understanding that they have access to both assertive and empathetic energies will empower them to use either style, whichever is most effective in a certain context, and to ignore the stigma connected with being "pushy" or "aggressive" when they employ assertive tactics. For men, accepting their empathetic side will enable them to employ more intuitive, compassionate approaches without judgment or prejudice.

In fact, I think reframing leadership along the lines of assertive and empathetic energies will be particularly powerful for men. Even if men want to be allies to women, they often don't know how to do so because they feel excluded from conversations about gender; they don't understand that they already have the tools they need for change and are equipped to take meaningful action.

Accepting that I have access to both approaches has helped me to unlock a new perspective and new skills in my leadership practice. From the moment I had my revelation, I have coached my teams and clients to do the same.

Leadership in Action

What does the integration of the two styles look like in practice? If you want to adopt this new way of exercising leadership—and empower others to do the same—you'll need to keep three things in mind:

1. Know Your Timing. Leadership is an art, not a science. This means you'll need to figure out day to day when to use a more assertive approach and when a more empathetic approach is more appropriate. One way to make this choice is to consider the differences between your role as a manager supervising functional roles and your role as a coach of human talent and potential. Nowadays, most leaders have to be both managers and coaches. Companies recognize this duality, and each role benefits from a different approach. Traditionally, the role of a manager has focused on the achievement of key performance indicators (KPIs) or targets. In fulfilling this part of your job description, which is results- and output-oriented, you might choose to use a more assertive, goal-oriented, and (moderately) competitive approach. On the other hand, companies increasingly understand the importance of coaching in shaping the workplace culture and overall performance of their organizations. A coaching role focuses less on outputs or outcomes and more on the holistic development of people—making sure they feel seen, heard, and understood so that they can confidently make decisions and feel committed to their teams. To be effective in this role, you might employ "softer" approaches, including listening and empathy.

2. Listen to What's Being Said and Not Being Said. You won't know which approach to use if you aren't attuned to the companies, communities, or teams that you want to mobilize or lead. That means understanding the culture of your group. Is there an imbalance in the way they approach tasks or challenges, over-favoring either assertive or empathetic energies? What is or isn't being said about the current norms of operating? What might you do in your role to facilitate a better integration of assertive and empathetic approaches, if an imbalance does exist? In your next meeting or group consultation, step back and observe what's going on in the room. Can you notice patterns in who is contributing to the discussion and who isn't? How about people's body language and behavior—what tends to get more air time? Predictable behaviors can be a sign of a predominant culture, one that may or may not be benefiting your group in their attempts to reach your objectives.

3. Be Open to Adapting When Things Don't Go as Planned. Employing both assertive and empathetic energies, and prizing both traits in your teams, will not always be easy, particularly given your own and other people's expectations and assumptions. Often the process will be wobbly and things won't go as planned. But there is no one right way to lead. Allow yourself to learn and adapt based on your objectives. That way, you won't risk pigeonholing yourself into one style of leadership or, more critically, lose your effectiveness and authority.

At some point in the past two chaotic years, I found that I had reached my maximum professional load. I was short-tempered and more aggressive, and I rushed from one thing to the next without giving myself time to think. Eventually, rather than trying to cover up what wasn't working and simply plow forward, I decided to sit down with my team and tell them that I needed their help in figuring out a new way to operate. By demonstrating my own vulnerability, I unintentionally allowed them to do the same. The meeting was immensely productive, and I wished I had held it much sooner. I encourage you to do in advance what I didn't: set aside time on a regular basis—whether weekly, monthly, or quarterly—to reflect on your leadership and assess objectively what has worked, what hasn't, and how you may need to adapt to changing circumstances.

Back to the Drawing Board

Now it was my counterpart's turn to sit and ponder. I don't think he had anticipated my question, assuming that I would give him a clear-cut answer. But then I asked my question: "Is women's leadership really any different from just plain old leadership? Or do you only think it has to be different?"

After a few moments of thought, he replied, "Hmm... I guess it doesn't have to be 'women's leadership.' I was thinking of one female supervisor who I had a bad experience with. But I know not all women are like that, and what she did isn't necessarily what all women leaders would do. I'm open to looking at 'just' effective leadership, regardless of whether it's male or female."

As we face more complex challenges at work, at home, and out in the world, our natural tendency is to retreat back to what is familiar, and to continue doing what's worked in the past, precisely because it has worked in the past. But it would be a disservice to our companies, communities, and ourselves not to think about how our past thoughts, actions, and beliefs might be limiting our future growth and transformation.

This gentleman was open to revisiting the way he looked at leadership. He realized that, instead of viewing "women's leadership" as ineffective, even damaging, he could embrace the fact that both men and women have access to any number of leadership tools.

If this one person was open to reframing his ideas, imagine what might happen if the same change in thinking occurred at scale. What possibilities will exist when we have left behind the divisive notion of "ourselves vs. others" and adopted the collaborative, integrated mindset of "ourselves and others"?

I hope we can get there.

"Feminism is nothing but equality, and actually, feminism benefits men because it liberates us and releases us from many stigmas imposed on us by the macho culture."

— Edgar Ramirez, Actor

| Chapter 03 |

How to Take Action
Through Women's Organizations And Communities

Daria Istrate
Harvard MBA
Consultant, Healthcare Sector

● ● ●

**Women in Positions of Power in Post-Communist
Countries: A Firsthand Account of a Romanian Woman
Immigrant**

I was born in 1985 in Communist Romania, to a family of
academics and intellectuals. The Iron Curtain fell for Romania on a
cold night in December of 1989, marking the cessation of a continuous, 42-year, authoritarian Communist regime.

I have only distant memories of what life used to be like back
then, but my parents grew up during those times. I remember dark
nights lit by gas lamps because electricity was provided on a limited
schedule; making sure to catch the dictator's broadcast on TV for a
couple of hours each day because that was the only thing you were
allowed to watch; my father tuning in secretly to "Radio Free Europe"
because the "Securitate" (Secret Romanian Police) would kidnap,

beat and sometimes kill you if you were caught listening to it. I also remember the systemic lack of food that forced my parents to wake up at 3 a.m. and stand in line for hours for basic necessities like bread, eggs, and toilet paper. In Maslow's hierarchy of needs, the ones at the very bottom—food and safety, personal security needs—were not covered. Anyone could be an informant: your friend, neighbor, priest, even your own spouse. There was no one to turn to for a safe conversation about how you felt. You were alone, especially if you had a brain. Intellectuals were ostracized by the regime; manual laborers were promoted.

This was the reality of my parents' youths, and it shaped them for life. The years were dark, and I was lucky to have experienced only a small number of them. That being said, you'd be surprised to find how many Romanians think life was better during Communism. Following the fall of the Communist regime, great fortunes were made through rampant corruption, illegal privatizations, massive restructurings, and fire sales of the industrial base. The IMF loan ballooned, and the Romanian real GDP contracted by 16% between 1989 and 2000.[1] Romanians went from living in a collectivist society in which most people were poor—but equal in their poverty—to a capitalist society in which the well-connected and the early entrepreneurs made fortunes and distanced themselves from the impoverished crowds. The country was undergoing tremendous change, and the very fabric of the society was changing rapidly, leaving many people stranded and disillusioned.

I grew up in Targoviste, a small town of roughly 70,000 people, located a 90-minute drive from Bucharest, the capital city. My parents are both high-school teachers, though my father was an

---

1   www.zf.ro/eveniment/romania-dupa-30-ani-economie-capitalista-10-ani-pierderi
-urmati-20-ani-crestere-economica-romania-inregistrat-cea-mare-crestere-economica-un
iunea-europeana-4-1-medie-an-an-perioada-2000-2019-18869921.

engineer by training; when his factory was closed, he became a Computer Science teacher. My mother is a History teacher, trained during the Communist regime. They have both worked for as long as I can remember, first as teachers and then, as they advanced in their careers, as leaders in local and regional educational institutions. My mother was a school principal for many years, and my father oversaw all the Computer Science teachers in the region.

Throughout my childhood, they continued to teach. I never kept close track of their career progression, but it was always clear to me that they were both hard-working, smart, and charismatic, and that their efforts were recognized through their increasingly prestigious positions. There was constant discussion at home about the fact that all public appointments were politically driven. Given that my parents never sided with either the social democrats or the liberals, they had to carry out a delicate dance of navigating the ever-changing regimes, at times unsuccessfully.

At home, my mother did all the chores—from cooking, grocery-shopping, and cleaning the house to traditionally "male" tasks like painting and fixing the toilet. I'm not sure how she managed to do it all while raising two children and working a full-time job, but she never complained, and it was understood, in the unwritten rules of Romanian families, that the woman would spend many hours every day in the kitchen while the children did their homework and the husband watched TV. Our home was no exception.

In high school, I started going to summer schools in Western European countries. I made German, Austrian, French, and Swiss friends and sometimes spent time living with their families. That was when I first realized that women in other countries experienced different work arrangements. Most of the women I encountered were stay-at-home moms; a rare few had worked part-time, but even then, it was always in education. Women's labor-force participation rate throughout Western Europe was below 40% in the 1990s.[2] Romania was different, with a more equal participation of women in the labor force: 46.5% post-Communism. Both adults in a household were usually income-earning. In Romania, the cost of living, coupled with the high inflation of the post-Communist era, was high compared to the average earning potential, which I believe played a large part in the country's gender dynamic.

This dynamic gave me a false sense of equality. I felt that Romania was different, that maybe this was one of the few good things to come out of Communism—a more egalitarian society, work for men and women alike. I did not question the ability of women (or men, for that matter) to become whatever they wanted in life. There was basically no difference in my mind between the sexes, in terms of what one could achieve with hard work and intellect.

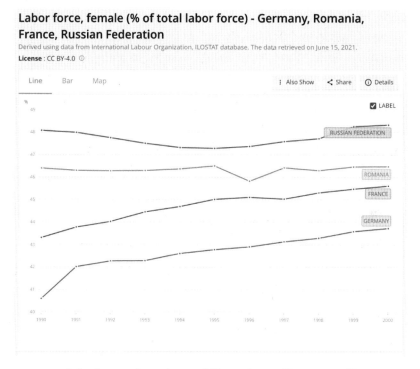

Labor force, female (% of total labor force) - Germany, Romania, France, Russian Federation

Derived using data from International Labour Organization, ILOSTAT database. The data retrieved on June 15, 2021.

License : CC BY-4.0 ⓘ

Moving to America and Pursuing a Corporate Career: The Nuances of Corporate America

I left my hometown when I turned eighteen and went to study International Economic Relations in Bucharest, then International Trade at the Sorbonne University in Paris. After graduation, I went into management consulting, a "work hard, play hard" environment with very ambitious, smart people whose main job is to advise the CEOs of multi-billion-dollar companies on big strategies with the potential to improve their businesses: market entry and exit strategies, restructuring initiatives, mergers & acquisitions, etc. My company was German, based out of Munich, and although most of the Partners (the highest level in the consulting hierarchy) were white men, I thought that was due to the strong legacy of the company's German founder and its relatively limited internationalization. In the Bucharest office, there were many women in entry-level and mid-management positions, and I even heard of a woman leading the office as Managing Partner (although that was before my time in the company). I never questioned the ability of talented women to become Partners if they worked really hard for it—and I did indeed encounter many talented and focused women. Yet, looking back at the ten years since I left the company, I notice that there are still very few women Partners.

The four years in strategy consulting equipped me with a good understanding of corporate life, in Romania in particular and in Europe more broadly. But I knew there was more to a career outside professional services, and I wanted to take a break from climbing the proverbial ladder and think about my next career move. I was fortunate to get accepted into Harvard Business School (HBS) to pursue my Master's in Business Administration (MBA).

I lived on campus in Boston for two years, between 2012 and 2014. In 2013, HBS celebrated fifty years of women in business education. The first women who had enrolled in the school were celebrated as true pioneers, who laid the groundwork for future generations of professional women. The MBA Class of 1965 had enrolled eight women, who represented less than 1% of the class. During my time at HBS, this number had grown to 40% of the MBA class, and it has continued to increase, with women representing close to 45% of the class of 2022.[3] At first, I didn't understand why the presence of women was such a big deal and needed to be celebrated.

My MBA class was diverse, with women from all over the world, including the Middle East, and women with very impressive pre-

---

3   HBS Statistics Overview Class of 2022 Enrollment, www.hbs.edu/about

MBA careers in investment banking, private equity, venture capital, strategy consulting—all competitive industries. Their contributions in the classroom were just as brilliant as those of their male counterparts, their aspirations just as high.

Then I started looking into the literature on women in corporate America, women in positions of senior leadership, equal pay, and gender diversity in the workplace. Despite important gains, women are still underrepresented in the corporate pipeline in the U.S. While women represented 48% of entry-level employees in 2021, that number was only 30% for the VP level and 24% for C-suite positions. The rhythm of gains over the 2016-20 period range from +1 percentage point for the VP level to +5 percentage points for the C-suite level.[4]

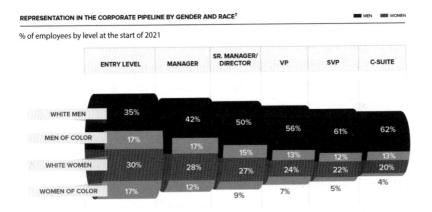

REPRESENTATION IN THE CORPORATE PIPELINE BY GENDER AND RACE[7]   MEN   WOMEN

% of employees by level at the start of 2021

These numbers indicate that, although women in America start their careers on a nearly equal footing to men, their progression doesn't happen at the same pace.

I have had an early-career experience in line with these statistics:

---

4   Women in the Workplace Report, 2021, McKinsey & Company.

fresh out of college, with limited family obligations, I perceived little to no difference between the women and men I worked with in consulting or interacted with during my MBA studies. As I advanced in my career journey, however, I observed more and more challenges faced by women in the workplace and came to understand how those challenge affect women's progression.

Challenges Faced by Women in the Workplace and Why It's Important to Act

1. The Elusive "Casual Intensity"

Many of the challenges that women face in the workplace are gender-specific and different from the ones men experience. The challenges may seem small at first, but they add up to such an extent that sometimes they result in career delays or an indefinite "layover" in a middle-management position. One issue that I myself have experienced in corporate America is being labeled "aggressive" and facing the potential penalty that comes with that label. I am a driven, ambitious, results-oriented, and very capable professional—and I wonder if a man with similar traits and aspirations would receive a similar label. I also come from a European culture that tends to be more direct, even blunt, than most Americans, and although I have spent the last ten years living and working in the U.S., some of that behavior still manifests itself. I tend to err on the side of assertiveness in my day-to-day interactions with my co-workers, bosses, and direct reports—a trait that is not traditionally expected from or associated with women in this country.

Traditional expectations are what trigger unconscious biases: social stereotypes about certain groups of people that individuals form outside their own conscious awareness.[5] Problems then arise when what people expect from others does not match the reality. For example, one might expect women to be warm and caring, men to be firm and decisive. One would then be taken aback by a woman who doesn't display a motherly instinct or, in my case, a woman who's very assertive.

What's frequently expected and rewarded in women, within the American corporate environment, is a "casual intensity" that combines hard work with fun. I was given this feedback with white gloves, wrapped in an overall positive communication that needed to be read between the lines. In fact, I had to look the phrase up because I had no idea what it meant. "Casual intensity" sounds good in theory, and it's something that's also rewarded in other parts of the world, but the way it is implemented in the U.S. and particularly on the West Coast is troublingly gender-specific. Men tend to have an easier time displaying and getting credit for the elusive "casual intensity," while still achieving their goals and being career-driven. For women, by contrast, displaying the right balance of hard work and fun is more difficult, if you want to avoid censure for being too "aggressive." It's something that I myself continue to work on.

2. Imposter Syndrome—Individual or Systemic?

A lot has been written about the imposter syndrome—feelings of self-doubt and personal incompetence that persist despite your education, experience, and accomplishments. A common reaction to this feeling is to work harder than anyone else, in order to get in front and prove yourself. I believe the syndrome can start early in childhood; at least it did for me. The general consensus in my family was

---

5   UCSF Office of Diversity and Outreach, diversity.ucsf.edu/resources/
      unconscious-bias.

that my brother was a genius, a world-class chess champion, whereas I did well in school because I was a hard worker. My older brother also did well in school when he applied himself, in spite of his busy schedule of training and competing. For him, however, academic excellence came with ease and was done as needed, while for me it was a full-time job and my sole focus.

Thirty years later, I am still battling the consequences of this family dynamic in my everyday life. Some may argue that it has translated into a solid work ethic, but I feel that with every new job, new role, or new promotion comes a lot of pressure to prove something (to myself; to the world; to both?) and that if I don't excel at every part of my job, I will betray the fact that I don't deserve to hold that position.

I believe that this problem is systemic rather than individual, and that women experience it more often than men. The familial dynamic I described—in which the son is deemed naturally talented while the daughter is viewed as excelling only through hard work—did not occur just in my family; it is something that many young girls grow up with and then need to overcome later in life. Usually the dynamic's effects are subtle, occurring in your subconscious, but it stays with you nonetheless, influencing you in ways that are often hard to identify.

3. The Historical Order of Things and the Force Required to Challenge the Status Quo

This discussion of gender-specific challenges is more relevant than ever, given how severely the Covid-19 pandemic has impacted women, who have reported increasing burn-out rates during the pandemic because of their greater burden in balancing the needs of their families with the requirements of working from home.

I work at Genentech, a biotechnology company based out of South San Francisco. We have a lot of women in senior leadership positions, and the opportunities for promotion are balanced across genders. The pandemic, however, had a visibly disproportionate impact on my women peers, who often had to take on more of the household responsibilities in their domestic lives, as compared with their husbands. Something had to give, so that each family could continue to function as a nucleus, with two working parents pursuing similarly demanding careers. The lack of daycare solutions and the extreme social isolation required all the families to create new solutions. I was happy to see that many of my female co-workers' male counterparts stepped up, splitting time during the workday so that they could help the children with homework and later on, when the children went back to school, taking turns to pick them up and drop them off. Although these new solutions have not entirely erased the woman's traditional role as the pillar of the household, they do represent a step in the right direction.

One positive impact of the pandemic is that advancements in virtual communication platforms have made connecting with other people much easier—the work-travel schedule and the daily commute no longer get in the way of holding meetings. External societies and support groups have thrived on virtual platforms as well, including many women's communities that have grown successfully in an all-virtual environment. As with all things pandemic-related, it is impossible to say for sure what will happen, but I believe this change might be here to stay, especially considering the benefits of being able to listen to virtual programming while also attending in-person meetings.

How to Be Part of the Conversation

As part of my research for this book, I reached out to several women leaders who are involved in women-led groups. I wanted to find out why they had joined these organizations and how their professional and personal lives changed as a result of their engagement. I also wanted to know how they think about the different support communities that are open to women. Should women plan to join one or several? Will joining a broader community of women solve their most pressing struggles? Are there still questions left unanswered?

I scheduled interviews with over fifteen mid-level and C-suite executives in finance, real estate, and healthcare—women in their thirties, forties, and fifties. They came from diverse ethnic backgrounds; some were daughters of recent immigrants, while others were immigrants themselves, and yet others came from families with a long American history. Some had been with the same company for more than ten years, while others had transitioned from multinational companies to startups and NGOs focused on local needs. Some were working moms with small children, while others had grown children or no children at all. One thing they all had in common, however, was their unanimous recognition of the positive impact generated by groups of women coming together and offering help, advice, connections, or just a willing ear.

One of the first things I learned through this research is that there are many women's organizations, all with different affiliations, all sharing the broader mission of supporting women in their careers and life journeys. While some are quite new and have grassroots origins, there's a clear trend among them toward institutionalization, with bigger employees starting to offer women-centered trainings as part of their corporate benefits.

The following is a non-exhaustive list of different types of women's groups accessible in the U.S.:

• **Alumni women's groups** (e.g. HBS Alumnae Circles). These are multi-generational groups with a shared school affiliation; women usually join them while in school and continue to attend long after graduation.

• **Industry women's groups** (e.g. Healthcare Business Association, How Women Invest). In these groups women share industry interests and expertise, and the conversations mostly center on how to navigate a particular industry, how to identify career opportunities, and how to gain expertise in certain areas.

• **Professional development / career advancement groups** (e.g. Chief, FirstBoard.io). These groups connect executive women with other women at similar career levels; they also help such women to find mentors.

• **Circles of interest** (e.g. Lean In Circles). In these groups, the topics range from the professional to the personal. They tend to be member-driven but guided by a trainer/coach, and are generally formed bottoms-up, in a decentralized fashion. Some have started collaborations with big corporations and are now offered to employees as part of their benefit packages.

• **Ethnic and cultural organizations** (e.g. Latinas in Tech). These groups are based on a common heritage and might bring together women who are at very different places in their careers.

Why Join?

When asked why they joined these organizations, the women I interviewed all gave surprisingly similar answers: the search for a higher purpose, the desire to form a deeper connection with other women, and the need to connect with people who were going through similar experiences. The women I spoke with are all high-powered individuals, leaders in their industries and respective organizations, mothers, wives, and pillars of their local communities. Though different in many ways, they all felt a strong need to talk to people facing gender-specific challenges: advancing in their careers as women, pregnancy, raising children, being working moms. For some, the urge to join came from a need for individual support—support limited to their own life and the decisions that they had to make for their own careers. For others, joining was part of a broader initiative of pushing for a more equitable workplace and striving to get and keep more women in positions of power.

I have been a member of the HBS Alumnae Circles for the last few years. The program started at the time of my graduation from HBS in 2014 and soon expanded to include over 2,000 alumnae across nine major regions (Boston, NYC, Washington DC, San Francisco City, San Francisco Peninsula, Austin, London, and Virtual/Houston). The mission of the program is to foster genuine relationships among HBS alumnae and to provide the opportunity for alumnae to learn from, support, and inspire one another both personally and professionally. I joined a six-member circle in San Francisco, and we met on a monthly basis for one year, usually for about two hours and usually at one of our houses; we would order dinner and chat in a casual environment. Our circle leader coordinated the logistics, and we soon settled into a routine. The group felt like a safe space to me, a space where authenticity and vulnerability were celebrated. The sessions' confidential nature made opening up easier.

Joining this group was a very pleasant experience for me, but commitment to it became difficult, due to my travel schedule and daily responsibilities. Nevertheless, this year I decided to take on a more active role and became a circle facilitator. Part of this decision came from my desire to create a space for more women to connect and bond. As I embark on this journey and kick off my first circle, I am excited to meet the members and share with them the norms and guidelines that will make this a pleasant and useful experience for all of us.

What Can You Expect to Gain from Your Engagement?

As the reasons for joining are specific to each person, so the impact of these groups is felt in many different ways. For most women, it's reassuring to be part of a group that speaks their language, deals with the same kind of challenges, and provides sound advice when needed. A supportive group can be an outlet to discuss problems, build relationships on a personal level, and reflect on your own experiences and how you might want to design or change your life.

The groups with members from different industries or different generations are particularly interesting because they tend to lead to "aha" moments that bring people closer together: "I am not alone. Others have been or are going through similar challenges, even though they don't work in the same field or are not the same age." Some women have compared sessions with their groups to shots of adrenaline, energy, positivity, and enthusiasm. Even when things do not go as planned in their own lives, members have found that being able to share their difficulties with a broader community of women makes things much easier.

Unfortunately, for women looking to drive change on a systemic level the road ahead is bumpier, and the results are often quite disappointing. It's empowering to set individual level goals—if you take ownership, develop the right plan, set up strategic meetings, etc., then your particular situation may improve— but how about fixing the larger places where women work, the systems in which women operate? This is a much more daunting task and requires a different type of broad engagement. Despite an ongoing, nation-wide interest in issues of gender experience and equity, the general opinion among the women I interviewed was that there hasn't been significant progress at a broad level over the past few decades, and that this lack of large-scale progress often hinders individual progress as well.

Which Type of Organization Should You Join and What Issues Will You Discuss?

Provided that you live in a part of the world with access to these types of organizations, finding the right one for you will be a journey of self-discovery. Each organization usually provides a mix of decentralized meetings and in-person programming. The bottoms-up meetings are often formed based on common areas of interest and are usually led by a coach whose remit is to guide the conversation and provide a safe space for members to share their experiences. The content is member-driven and can range from very personal discussions to big structural issues. Some of the trending topics include:

- Transitioning back into the workplace
- Planning your work/life balance
- Making time for yourself
- Learning new skills
- Developing and nurturing a support network
- Leveraging social media to act powerfully
- Increasing engagement at work, at home, socially, and in the community
- Developing a vision for what your legacy will be
- Pursuing your personal passion or side hustle

The meetings are usually robust, with people opening up in the small-group environment. While it can be harder to make friends and develop deep connections as we age, members of women's groups report quickly reaching a level of comfort that allows them to discuss anything from marriage problems to career conversations. The programming is open to all members and answers the need of self-actualization outside the daily job. Some organizations offer talks from senior leaders on how to run a company, the challenges they had to face along their career journey, the traps that women fall into when trying to balance work and life, etc.

If you can't find any groups nearby, search online and see if you can join a community in another region or country. You can also take the initiative and create your own local group. Websites like Lean In (www.leanin.org/) provide a lot of information on how to set up and run your own circle of women. They offer free resources for who to invite to your circle, how to communicate with the group's members, how to schedule and run successful meetings, how to moderate the discussions, how to set clear goals, and even how to provide online trainings for anyone interested. Developing these skills may come in useful in your day-to-day job too, by helping you to demonstrate leadership and develop your skills in coordinating a group of people and guiding them toward a specific goal.

What Still Needs to Be Done?

The women I interviewed all agreed that there is still a long road ahead, with much change and progress still to be made. Some of the issues they brought up pertain to national policy and systems that need to be established to enable women to break out of behavioral patterns that have been in place for decades, particularly the convention of a woman being the anchor-person at home. The interviewees especially emphasized the need to balance work and family life, to encourage true co-parenting, and to encourage technology solutions.

One topic of interest was the need for active involvement from men in these discussions and a recognition that meeting as a women-only group may create an echo-chamber that lacks a diversity of perspective. Most women want to be challenged in their beliefs and would embrace having an open dialogue with their male counterparts. A closer collaboration would also provide a solid grounding for men as they strive to build diversity within their own organizations, using their positions of power.

Many of the women called for clearer metrics for tracking progress and establishing accountability. These metrics could be adapted by each organization and even rolled out on a national scale. Broader goals could be instituted, like increasing the number of women gaining an MBA by a certain percentage each year or volunteering a hundred hours a year to educating and mentoring younger women.

Within the workplace, KPIs (Key Performance Indicators) often do not take into account the systemic and institutionalized biases still affecting many companies. We've all read or heard about the stereotypes that women and men fall into: women are "bossy," men are "decisive"; women who are ambitious and assertive are "unlikeable, even "bitchy," while women who fit their gender stereotype by being gentle and caring are "not leadership material." This is called the "likeability" problem, and it's been shown to impact performance reviews, hiring decisions, and promotions. Building a recognition of this problem into KPIs would certainly improve the overall conditions for women in the workplace.

Takeaways

For me, the most important takeaway from my research was that, with all the demands on our time and our lives, it is important to set aside mental and physical space to reflect, and also to be an active participant in your own life. Women's groups and communities can help you in this process. We should all take the time to identify and engage with the right group(s), and always remember that we're not alone!

I also believe that change starts with each one of us. One of my mentees is an East Asian leader whose goal is to become a C-Suite Executive at her company. She also wants to start a family and is going through IVF treatment. We've had many discussions about how to maintain a work-life balance, how and if you can advance in your career while raising a family, and how having children might impact our career ambitions and timelines. Our most recent chat was about a former woman employee who was a top performer at my mentee's company but felt obliged to quit work altogether in her efforts to have children. Fortunately, she conceived soon after she left the company and was ready to come back after a leave of absence of eighteen months. Before doing so, she asked to downshift her position to Assistant Manager so that she could take care of her family at the same time. However, my mentee had a limited headcount, and she needed to hire someone for a Manager position.

Although we had discussed how women need to be empowered in the workplace, we both found ourselves wondering how rehiring the former employee might impact the business, and we discussed the risks associated with taking a leap of faith. We brainstormed about splitting her responsibilities with another peer or setting up a one-year pilot program to see how the employee managed her work/life balance. In the end, certain accommodations were made so that the employee could return to work and even get promoted to Manager. I remained struck by how self-aware this ambitious employee had been in asking for a downshift in her responsibilities. Although the person responsible for rehiring her was also a woman, the decision was not straightforward. This was not a reflection on the hiring manager—it was just an inevitable result of the need to balance professional and personal obligations.

I asked some of my interviewees to provide a message to the next generation of women professionals, in their twenties and early thirties, who might be dealing with some of these challenges and thinking about joining a women's group. Here's what they told me:

- "No matter what you do, it's hard to do it alone, so it's important to find a group that will support and meet your needs. These are not extracurricular activities; it is part of your job to build these networks outside your organization." *(Rosa Ziebell, VP of Marketing at the Sheryl Sandberg & Dave Goldberg Family Foundation)*

- "Find what works for you." *(Kate Rowbotham, VP of Customer Engagement at Genentech)*

- "Every successful person has a really powerful network behind them. Carve out time to connect with a group of people who have your interests at heart and who will give you frank feedback." *(Christine Cordato, Managing Director at Crescente Advisors)*

- "We tend to overprepare and don't really need all of that. We have unique experiences and perspectives that we can apply without all the certifications and such. It's not as hard as you think." *(Erika Cramer, Managing Member and General Partner at How Women Invest)*

• "You get what you put into it and sometimes more. Just showing up matters: be there, participate, keep trying and showing up, be more action-oriented than just saying, 'I should do that…' You have to make time and show up now, not tomorrow. You need to create the time and space to do it." *(Cindy Park, COO at Prado Group)*

• "Don't be so isolated and think that your issues are unique. So many of us struggling with similar situations—there's that power of sharing and relating." *(Cindy Park, COO at Prado Group)*

| Chapter 04 |

Piercing through the 3 Headwinds
for Working Women

Nikita Jain
Founder & CEO, Eubrics

● ● ●

"I'm sorry," Priya said, visibly distressed. "I have my limitations, so I cannot take up this new role."

Concerned and unable to get over my surprise, I said, "You do realize that we are grooming you for leadership and that this is a high-paying, fast-growth role in a new country, where you can make a mark."

"I can't," she mumbled, almost in tears.

"Can you help me understand what your real apprehension is?" I asked. "The reason you shared on email—that you're 'not feeling ready'—didn't sound as if it came from the Priya I know, the woman who's been so outspoken about her hunger to take on new challenges."

After some hesitation, Priya said, "It would mean that my husband would have to look for another job, since I would be earning twice what he does. In our family, it's unacceptable for a woman to have a better-paying job than her husband. I have to prioritize family over career."

With these words, she left the room.

It was a summer afternoon in June 2015, and I had just concluded a coaching session with one of my clients, a senior leader in a global technology company. Her final explanation left me speechless and caused an array of memories to flood into my mind.

I am a woman from a socioeconomic background similar to Priya's. We had been pleasantly surprised to discover that our formative years were spent in neighboring areas of New Delhi, India. But I still struggled to explain why she was prepared to jeopardize her dreams and everything she had worked so hard for in order to 'prioritize family over career.' I wondered if her husband would ever find himself placed in a similar situation—and if he did, would he choose his family over his career?

This chapter focuses on the three main challenges for women pursuing professional careers in India and, more broadly, Asia: (1) decision surrogacy, (2) lack of sponsorship, and (3) what I call the Do-It-Yourself Syndrome. These are challenges that I've experienced myself, that I've observed in cases like the one described above, and that I've discussed while leading gender-diversity programs and coaching sessions for women professionals.

The Roots

I was born into a traditional North Indian, middle-class, merchant family. While my father was expected to manage the family business, his early education helped him form an aspiration to join the government service. He wanted to contribute meaningfully to a newly independent India. So, resolutely, he pushed aside his destined path and followed his dream. Growing up, his strong rejection of the word 'impossible' was always evident to me. Discussing ways to plan well and make things happen was a common dinner-table activity for us. I wasn't allowed to complain; instead, I was expected to think of methods for making my situation better. I recollect his standard response to every challenge I shared: "Things don't happen on their own; if you want something, you'd better be prepared to work for it." At that point, I didn't know that he was training my sisters and me to tackle all the challenges and societal stereotypes that work against women.

My mother served as my first female role model, actively balancing her family commitments with her life interests. She is a home-maker with varied interests and has a deep reservoir of resilience that has served all of us well in times of adversity. I used to share everything that happened in school with her, but it never occurred to me to ask how she reconciled her keen intellect and diverse interests with being a 'conventional' home-maker. She found her own ways to channel her superior problem-solving skills, whether by helping my father think through his options in sticky work situations or by resolving quarrels amongst her bickering children.

I grew up seeing my parents work as a team, with no visible gender segregation of chores or tasks. My father used to wake up early to help my mother in the kitchen, and she often discussed his work challenges with him. They extended this homogeneous approach to their children, never applying a gendered lens to our upbringing. This was especially empowering considering that the majority of Indian parents typically consider their daughters' education as a means to find great marriage prospects for them. In our house, by contrast, it was all candid conversations about working hard and creating independent careers for ourselves. "Can girls fly planes?" I asked as a curious seven-year-old. My mother replied, "There is nothing in this world that girls can't do. They can fly planes, administer nations, and even create life!"

The notion that education and vocation are not bracketed by gender took deep root in my mind. In this way I was unlike many of my female classmates and friends, who were steered towards 'women-compatible professions' like teaching, clerical work, and office administration. Women in India are seen primarily as home-makers and are conditioned to adopt a 'family-first' approach to their own lives. Growing up, I saw my women friends and cousins being encouraged to prioritize stability over risks, even if the risks offered potentially greater opportunities, and to prefer pre-set patterns over active decision-making. Yet such choices often lead to deep (and, sadly, seldom talked about) dissatisfaction and a lack of self-worth over time.

I have encountered this dissatisfaction again and again in my coaching conversations with professional women, such as the one I had with Priya. In our society, women are prepared to fit one specific role: home-maker. But many women do not follow this trend, and those who don't—those who take jobs outside the home—need more than just mentors or advisors; they need tools that will empower them and help them make their own decisions. Here's my single advice to manage the perpetual guilt as you access the special organizational resources/programs to support women professionals: *No, they don't give you an unfair advantage, they simply level the field for you (to some extent!).*

1. Decision Surrogacy

This brings me to the first major stumbling block for professional women in India: what I call 'decision surrogacy.' Not having the moral support—or even the basic skills—to make the decisions that affect their own lives is one of the key barriers to success for women in

India. Typically, male surrogates in the family—fathers, brothers, or husbands—make these critical decisions on their female relatives' behalf.

Men make decisions for women 'beginning with whether they will be allowed to be born. This is followed by every life decision, including education and marriage.'[1] In 2021, LXME interviewed 1,250 women aged 25 to 54 in Mumbai, Bengaluru, New Delhi, Mangalore, Pune, Jaipur, Kolkata, Indore, and Hyderabad. Out of all the married women interviewed, 69% were not making independent financial decisions; their fathers' financial power was later replaced by that of their husbands or by joint decision-making.[2] Growing up, I observed this trend firsthand, both at school and among my work friends, who were guided completely by their families on what educational paths they should pursue, what jobs they should take up, and what men they should marry.

In contrast, my parents offered guidelines rather than rules. Very early, they made me take on some of the critical decisions affecting my own life. More often than not, having to do so felt quite unsettling, given that those decisions had a real-life impact. "I'd like to study engineering, but only four girls in my class are even applying to engineering colleges," I told my father one evening. He replied immediately, "The question is not whether you—a girl—should apply or not. The question is whether you have it in you to succeed as an engineer."

Though intimidating at the time, my parents' insistence that I take my life into my own hands and become accountable for my own decisions ultimately brought me success and a satisfactory career.

---

1   www.tandfonline.com/doi/full/10.1080/10130950.2021.1958549.
2   www.businessinsider.in/thelife/news/66-single-women-do-not-make-own-financial-decisions-new-survey-reveals/articleshow/79621626.cms.

Thanks to their early encouragement, I took up a consulting job with a multi-national corporation and worked with CEOs and CHROs on honing their leadership practices and strategies. The work required frequent travel and long working hours, but it also helped me understand and experience my own potential as a professional and, more importantly, as a working woman.

As I was diving into this job, many of my friends were dropping off the career radar at the 'ideal marriageable age' of 24. The high percentage of working women who drop out of the workforce to get married was shown statistically in 2017 in a McKinsey report on Women in the Workplace. According to the report, women of color represent 18% of the entry-level workforce worldwide, but this number is reduced to only 3% at the C-suite level.[3] Such a dramatic drop in percentage represents the impact of decision surrogacy on working women.

In my career I have often found myself in a lonely struggle to grow and be successful, because I didn't have many women role models who could teach me how to handle critical life issues as a professional woman—issues such as marriage, children, and relocation. I had to rely mostly on my own judgment to make many intimidating, life-altering decisions, and I did so while taking into consideration the necessities of my career.

Such life decisions often present critical turning points for working women like Priya. Women tend to lean towards the decisions favored by their family, or to prioritize their husbands' careers over their own, thanks to the lack of guidance from other women or any prior experience that might help them make informed decisions prioritizing their own careers.

---

3   www.mckinsey.com/featured-insights/gender-equality/still-looking-for-room-at-the-top-ten-years-of-research-on-women-in-the-workplace

Given the societal pervasiveness of decision surrogacy, what would really help working women in Asia (including me) is our own version of the Old Women's Club, which would give us access to women role models, women-led opportunities, and women organizational sponsors.

2. Lack of Sponsorship

This brings me to the next major stumbling block for professional women in India: a lack of sponsorship. Even with a strong will and determined attitude, one of the most difficult career challenges for Indian working women is a dearth of advocacy and confidence in them from their organizations and families. The majority of women are not allowed to decide on their own career or to work at all after marriage. Those women who do keep their professional positions often end up working doubly hard simply to be on par with their male colleagues, while also shouldering a disproportionate load of family commitments.

The outcome is that women like Priya frequently refuse to take on more challenging roles or promotions at work. Many of the women I coach feel enormous guilt because of their professional travel requirements and late working hours—hours that their children and families spend without them at home. Indian society multiplies these burdens with its intergenerational living culture: often a married woman will live with her children, her husband, and his family, including his parents, siblings, and grandparents. Such large households add immeasurably to the expectations for women. They also add to the limitations on a woman's ability to control her own spending and her economic freedom, since there are so many family members eager to decide how and when her earnings should be spent to meet the family's expenditures. Most of the times, women are left with no time to build sponsors who can advocate and help them grow into senior, complex roles.

On my first day as a working woman, I walked into the office with mixed feelings of excitement and fear. It was my first job, and I desperately needed guidance. Then I met my team and my new manager in the cafeteria, and they told me how proud they were to hire me. I had worked very hard to get to this point, and it put me at ease to be recognized for my merit (believe me, we all crave that recognition!). My academic credentials had brought me this far, but I knew that in the journey ahead I would need constant support and empowerment from both the organization I worked for and my family.

Soon I started observing the much-talked-about gender stereotypes in the workplace: the boys' clubs offering an abundance of male mentors and supporters, and the active networking among men at after-office parties. I wanted to break into these circles without losing my innate identity as a woman, and I started exploring my options. What intuitively came to me was powerful: the concept of sponsorship.Gaining one or more sponsors is a way for women to build credibility that transcends gender and offers a potentially constant source of support for working women.

I have been interested to see that the tactic I instinctively pursued in 2011 has now become celebrated, advocated, and discussed in depth over the past few years. In a corporate world, sponsorship for women is a real game-changer, one that can empower women in the face of all the societal headwinds.

Here's a description of what sponsorship means:

"Mentors help you skill up, sponsors help you move up"
by beleaderly.com[4]

In my own career, I have worked very hard and persistently towards building a circle of sponsors both at home and at work. At home, I was fortunate to have both my parents and my husband as willing supporters. However, turning them into my sponsors took much more time, effort and patience. Throughout my consulting career, I used to travel a lot and to work late nights and weekends. My days became even more demanding when I started my entrepreneurial journey. I was always conscious of discussing and co-planning my crazy schedules, financial situation, and personal choices with my husband. Even today, it is not easy, our realities, expectations and plans keep changing. What helps is our constant dialogue and the inner courage to discuss and reason out the options I have, the best ways to balance my work needs with my family commitments. These conversations are not always easy, but they certainly help my family understand what is important to me and makes me a happier, more contented human being.

At work, I stretch myself and do my best to deliver every single time. Each day comes with constant performance pressure, and I have always had to find ways to exceed expectations. For a woman, the field is not level; I've had to do more to prove my credibility and commitment than my men colleagues. As Charlotte Whitton, Mayor of Ottawa, once said, "Whatever women do they must do twice as well as men to be thought half as good. Luckily, this is not difficult." For me the hard work has been rewarding, and it earned me ongoing support from the organizational leaders who I never thought would become my sponsors.

Multiple times, early on in my career, I ran into ingrained gender stereotypes with my clients, but these were the times when I could experience the power of authentic connections and sponsorship.

---

4   www.theleadershipinstitute.com.au/2019/12/women-need-career-sponsors/.

During a project for a power-sector company, the client, objecting to my assignment to the project, announced, "Girls cannot work at plants, so we would like a male consultant." My leader replied, "She is the best we have." I continued on the project and completed it successfully, with high client ratings at its close. But sponsorship didn't exist from Day 1. I remember when I first met this leader, I generally discussed my goals and challenges at work. It started with him being a mentor. But over time, with my continuous work commitment and performance, he observed my potential and we built trust that transformed him automatically to be my sponsor. And, then he was undeterred by such stereotypes, he assigned me numerous projects and opportunities, based on my merit.

It is also noteworthy that my leaders gave me tremendous support during significant changes in my personal life, such as when I got married, struggled with my father's diabetic condition, and juggled family commitments. They consistently offered their support, helped me find doctors, and—first and foremost—offered me deep empathy at work. At this point, I would like to re-emphasize that there is a severe dearth of women sponsors for the working women. Many of my women coachees expressed their discomfort with reaching out to male leaders for their sponsorship. However, I have personally worked with both male and female sponsors, and to me, as long as your sponsor values your skills, and stands up for you, it is all good.

Sponsorship is widely advocated for women leaders today, but, as I found in my own experience, it is an ongoing process and not a panacea for every problem. As I took on more challenging roles and advanced in my career, the expectations at work and at home kept increasing. Even today I must juggle my priorities, letting go of some opportunities at work for my family and vice-versa. Nevertheless, sponsorship has proven to be the most powerful tool I've had as I pursue my evolving professional and personal goals. To me, what's especially interesting is the beautiful amalgamation of the two worlds, work and home, as my sponsors come together to propel me. My work sponsors support me during times of personal difficulty, and my family sponsors stand by me when my work demands become overwhelming.

3. The Do-It-Yourself Syndrome

Working women tend to do things alone, and in the process, they often feel lonely and isolated. This phenomenon is what I call the Do-It-Yourself Syndrome, and it is common even in India, despite the social conditioning of Asian women to stay focused on relationships and build ties to keep their families united. The journey of leadership is all about building great relationships and being an inspiration for the people. Networking, delegating, and leveraging relationships at work are all ways of mitigating the DIY Syndrome for professional women.

In my own career, I found the concept of relationship-building particularly intriguing. Coming from a 'can do' upbringing, I always believed that I could get anything done myself if I worked hard enough, and this belief was reinforced by my strong academic achievements. But things changed after I began to work. I was constantly surprised by how often the rewards and resources allotted at my workplace were distributed based on who had built the right relationships. Quickly embarking on new projects, executing ideas, even validating another's idea is easy for those who can act with a simple phone-call. This reality is true for both men and women, but their responses to it, in my experience, are different.

Building effective, functional relationships was a bigger challenge for me and my fellow women colleagues than for my male associates. In multiple conversations with other women leaders, I have discover-

ed that when it comes to building networks and leveraging relationships, women in India face a values-based conflict. They are deeply
conditioned to be the givers in every relationship, and thus, when
they act in an assertive, outcome-driven way, they are often labeled as
bossy. This result creates a conflict between their self-view of being
outcome-driven and the external obligation of being empathetic and
giving. Irrespective of their achievements, professional women are
consistently evaluated on their ability to demonstrate empathy and
care. In 2018, in a global employee survey conducted by one of my
organizations, the characteristics of high performers were different for
men and for women in India. High-performing men were associated
with their drive for achievement, while high-performing women were
associated with their relationships and level of care for others.[5]

While I was ambitious in my career, as an Indian girl I felt deeply
connected with the fundamental values of being empathetic and a
giver. I grew up drawing deep inspiration from my elder sister, Mansi.
She has always been the caring one, taking into consideration everyone's opinions and always putting herself in others' shoes. She served
as a model for me, teaching me how to care deeply, and I applied this
model with my teams, clients, and managers in order to build trust
and deep relationships.

My struggle was to balance my natural outcome-oriented person
-ality with my instinct for empathy. Often, I ended up having to
choose one or the other and then felt dissatisfied with people's perception of me. I wanted to solve this dilemma, so I spoke to male
colleagues, mentors, and team-members, trying to balance empathy
and ambition so that I could build functional relationships. During
this process I realized that, as a woman with Indian values, the task
posed barriers at multiple, unexplored levels for me. I had to be

5   Internal survey outcome by one of the global consulting firms in 2017

vulnerable, ask for help, and let go of my constant need to be perfect, in order to align others with my goals. These necessities seemed scary because of their potential impact on my credibility, which I had earned through years of sacrifice, balancing acts, and hard work. On the other hand, continuing with inadequate and weak relationships would have impaired the growth of my team and my career. So, in the end, I chose vulnerability.

My formula for success was to share my plans honestly and seek support from others. I complemented these tactics with my talent for being empathetic and approachable, so that others could seek my support without any fear of losing status. These strategies helped me to establish mutual expectations clearly and respectfully.

The real potential of these relationships unfolded for me when I started my own company, Eubrics.com, a behavioral nudge platform that offers gamified development journeys profiled as per psychometric analysis of each employee.

With real-time job actions and feedback nudges daily, Eubrics help employees share and acquire the desired behaviors in a measurable and sustainable way. It improves the productivity and job outputs of employees. It shapes the culture and communities of an enterprise. When I became the CEO of Eubrics, I had never felt so strapped for resources and time. Moreover, my mentors warned me of the biases that prevail in the industry regarding women founders and their life choices, commitment level, business skills, and networks. The existence of these biases has been confirmed by global research and the observations of seasoned women entrepreneurs.[6] Given this uneven playing field, I knew it was critical to be ready from Day One.

In my preparations, I gathered perspectives, support, and advice

---

6   www.orfonline.org/research/women-entrepreneurs-in-india-what-is-holding-them-back-55852/.

from my network; several colleagues introduced me to their connections in the start-up world. Starting from zero, I soon gathered valuable insights through conversations and advice from other founders, industry experts, customers, and product users across the globe. Simultaneously, I worked on strengthening the inside core of the company i.e., my team. I shared my vulnerability as a CEO openly, though initially I was scared to lose my credibility as a leader and worried that my honest might diminish my team's morale and trust in Eubrics. In the end I avoided these pitfalls by creating a robust business plan that offered a safety-net to my team and the company. We defined clear goals and milestones that were achievable. Over time, working in an open culture, my team realized that they could express their vulnerability and concerns freely. We worked through our initial guesswork about each other and ended up functioning as a reliable, trusting unit. We had come a long way, simply from working together and collaborating to push forward our company's vision.

With this well-oiled machinery I was able to prove Eubrics' mettle in the most debated areas for women founders: networks, commitment, and business outcomes. My team achieved stellar results in product development, market validation, and sales in just six months, creating a fully tested, seamless product with of over twenty modules, validated by over fifty CEOs and CHROs, in trials and projects with over fifteen organizations. This was made possible by five talented people, each stalwart and deeply committed to Eubrics' mission of enabling enterprises to achieve the highest potential and output of every working professional. As we strove to achieve our goals, we debated, laughed, and brainstormed together, coming up with unlikely and innovative ideas to build Eubrics.

For women founders or leaders who are trying to build successful businesses and organizations, it is crucial to build up a network of people who believe in your vision, are willing to become a part of your team, and will offer you unconditional support. Women leaders must leverage empathy and focus on relationships to build authentic connections. With these tools and a steadfast ambition, the possibilities for women are endless in today's world, where we can connect, learn, and share with people across the globe.

Sum and Substance

My discussion with Priya helped me to process my own experiences as an Indian working woman. To help her work through her choices, I shared some of my observations, including the top five myths that limit women leaders, both in India and globally, and my suggestions for counteracting them:

Myth 1: Ambition is a Bad Word

Women are often labeled as bossy or impatient when they display leadership characteristics that are associated with drive and success in men. Dream big and chase your goals without worrying about these labels. For me, ambition fuels perseverance and resilience. It helps me believe that I deserve the success I'm seeking. Verbalize your desire, and you will see it becoming more real in your own and others' minds. This strategy will help you to overcome derogatory labels and enable you to garner support and take on more challenging opportunities at work.

Myth 2: Perfection Is the Only Way to Succeed

The biggest roadblock that I have observed for Asian women leaders is their tendency to insist on perfecting something, while men raise their hands even if they are only partially ready. Research from

---

7   www.hbr.org/2014/08/why-women-dont-apply-for-jobs-unless-theyre-100-qualified.

Harvard indicates that women often lack the self-confidence to apply for jobs for which they don't see themselves as 100% qualified.[7] It is important to start evaluating your opportunities beyond the rule book. Skills like relationship-building, drive, and communication can make women ideal candidates for big opportunities at work. Constant learning and hard work are essential for both men and women.

Myth 3: You Cannot "Have It All"

Research proves that women are great jugglers. I use this skill all the time to stay productive and energized. As I work towards success, I simultaneously admire the beauty of trees and plants, learning lessons of evolution and adaptability from them. My personal and coaching experiences with other women have helped me realize that most women can plan, think, and execute multiple tasks at one time—in short, they can "have it all." Use this to your advantage!

Myth 4: Your Networks Cannot Be a Part of Your Career Journey

Bosses, friends, family, and other women can serve as a much-needed support system and share your life decisions. There are so many social networks for women available today, enabling women to connect with and support each other. As a woman who has battled with varied career challenges, I feel that my journey has benefited from significant contributions from supportive friends, relatives, and colleagues. Find your advocates, counselors, and motivators throughout your career, and offer the same help to other women. Make time to stay in touch and build deeper relationships with them.

Myth 5: Taking 'Me Time' Is Selfish

Many women I have met are conditioned by their societies to think of others before themselves. They feel guilty when they take time away for their own comfort. But I have realized the hard way that life is a marathon, and refueling frequently is key to survival. This is true for both men and women leaders. For that reason, the field must be leveled when it comes to taking personal time. My simple trick to gain 'me time' is to divide my goals into small, achievable milestones. This helps me become more productive and make time for my own health and hobbies. I have a daily workout built into my schedule to stay physically fit. I keep time for traveling because it is revitalizing to draw inspiration from other cultures, art, and people. 'Me time' is a golden opportunity for women to zoom out and celebrate their own journeys.

This chapter has been about my personal experiences of the challenges that confront professional Indian women, and Asian women generally, as they prepare for and achieve their career goals while also balancing their personal priorities. Becoming a leader as a woman will never be a fairy tale with one happy ending; on the contrary, it will be a constant pursuit with many victories and failures. According to McKinsey's recent research, today's workplaces require flexibility and soft skills for success.[8] Fortunately, these trends offer fresh opportunities for women professionals to balance their priorities and pursue desirable careers.

As I conclude this chapter, feeling an onslaught of realizations, reflections, and nostalgia, I hope that you will connect with and find

---

8   www.mckinsey.com/featured-insights/gender-equality/the-future-of-women-at-work-transitions-in-the-age-of-automation.

| Chapter 05 |

A Woman Wearing Many Hats:

Leadership and Allyship from the Standpoint of a
Married Woman with Children

Jane Jiyoung Park
Musician, Entrepreneur & Mother of Three

●●●

Prologue

It was August 14, 1998, in Pohang, South Korea. My mom had just parked the car around the corner from a student dormitory at Handong University. We strolled toward the place where we were scheduled to meet a young man who had called my aunt two weeks earlier. My family and I were in transition, relocating from Los Angeles to Seoul. According to my aunt, the student who was meeting us would be polite and friendly, sharing information about the university's orientation week in early September. Finally, the day had come for us to meet him, and I looked forward to going on our campus tour and learning about university life.

The young man stood in a hallway by the university's entrance, a neatly dressed student with carefully combed hair, expecting us. When he saw us, he approached with a big smile on his face. My mom and I found him professional and well-mannered. As he led us around, I grew more and more excited. Here I was in Pohang, on the southeastern tip of the Korean peninsula, a well-known seaport and home to one of the world's largest steel mills. This was where I would live for the next four years.

Two weeks later, it was the first day of school. As I hurried toward my second class after lunch, I saw the young man again. He smiled and asked how I was doing. In the days to come our paths crossed frequently, as several of our classes took place in the same building. Every time I bumped into him, he was lively and lighthearted, and he always wore a big smile. We quickly realized that we were interested in each other.

Exactly seven years later, on September 20, 2005, we became engaged, and our wedding took place two months later, on November 5. Now, seventeen years later, I am forty-one, a wife and the mother of three beautiful children. My husband and I realized earlier this year that we have known each other for close to two thirds of our lives—twenty-four years of both blissful and challenging times, experienced together. As a woman of the Christian faith, I believe it is by God's grace that we are still thriving today, side by side.

In this chapter, I wish to share some reflections, opinions, and suggestions on the topics of leadership, allyship, and gender from the standpoint of a married woman with children.

Humans Can't Survive Without Relationships and Allyships

Let's be straight: humans are social animals. We can't survive on our own; we need to mingle with others, whether we are introverts or extroverts. We call such bonds relationships. But relationships are not effortless; they require a commitment, a genuine effort to nurture the connection by building trust. Any bond of this kind requires time and resources in order to become healthy and robust. With the right care, a good relationship can turn into an even better allyship, in which two people support each other and promote each other's success. Husband and wife, parents and children, teacher and students, superior and subordinate, spiritual leader and congregations—these can all be examples of powerful allyships, if the relationships are supportive and healthy.

Personally, I have had some trouble developing and nurturing relationships in my life. By nature, I am a people person: I value friendship, rapport, and trust. However, because I have moved around a lot since childhood, going from one country to another first because of my father's occupation as a TV reporter and later because of my husband's frequent relocations for work, I have experienced constraints on developing deep and prolonged relationships.

Allyship was even tougher for me, because I found it difficult to share my personal convictions and aspirations with others. I never knew when I would be saying good-bye to the people I was with, and naturally I felt more comfortable listening than speaking. But, in recent years, I have realized that relationships and allyships are critical to human existence, helping us survive in an ever more complex and challenging environment, and I have tried hard to create more of them in my own life.

Everyone on earth is currently experiencing unprecedented challenges, intense volatility, and increasing uncertainty from both within and outside. These challenges and uncertainties range from job insecurity and health vulnerabilities to political upheaval, social unrest, and economic downturns. As a result, adaptability has become a hyper-critical trait for all of us. It is both a mindset and a skill, and it must be practiced by everyone. At the same time, relationships and allyships have become even more important, as they can help us enormously in navigating uncertainty. Robust partnerships at every level, in families and in workplaces, can enable us to become strong and effective leaders with the power to survive and thrive as a community.

Of course, forging partnerships and becoming an effective leader are not simple tasks. I find that promoting allyship at home, between husband and wife, is one of the toughest challenges of all, though also the most rewarding. Here are my observations and reflections on why this is so.

Reflection 1 – Accept that Everyone Is Different, But Let This Be an Asset

After getting married, my husband and I were surprised to learn that we shared many more things in common than we had originally realized. At the same time, our differences were exposed in greater magnitude.

We both love people, traveling, music, sports, children, and working for our community. Both of were raised globally. We have each lived and traveled in many countries, eighty in the case of my husband. Both of us, and our children as well, love music, playing different instruments and singing at home and in church.

On the flipside, our differences were startling. I grew up with two other siblings, both girls. I was quiet, girlish, an indoor type. Our mom tried to raise all three of us in an elegant way, especially during our time in Paris, France. My husband, by contrast, grew up as what he calls a "jungle boy." As a child of humanitarian workers, living in rural areas of the Philippines and other countries in the Pacific region, he was almost never at home, instead spending his days in trees and on hills and streams, carrying out a child's version of expeditions.

We all have different upbringings, with different exposures, experiences, and education. When two people come together as husband and wife, they need to understand from the beginning that they are different, and that it may not be easy to form a team and navigate a life path jointly. Because of their inevitable differences, two people in a marriage often form and hold very different value systems, and even have different interpretations or definitions of shared values. For example, my definition of success is linked to the present, while for my husband it focuses on the future. He is willing to sacrifice some benefits in the present for the sake of a better future, while I feel that what we do today is the most important factor.

Such differences will inevitably affect how people teach their children and what values they emphasize as important. The question of how we should use our limited resources, including our time, money, energy, and effort, will inevitably be contingent on the values we uphold. In the early days of our marriage, and also in the rearing of our children, my husband and I have experienced tensions surrounding our different understandings of important values, even those we shared.

Personality is another significant element of allyship to consider. While I would describe myself as reserved, diagnostic, and risk-averse, my husband is confident, risk-taking, determined, and energetic. These aspects of his personality have troubled me at times, as our expectations have often been misaligned. Sometimes he has made things happen without giving me enough time to examine the situation and make an informed judgment; often dramatic events in our lives have happened unexpectedly and simultaneously. Naturally, this kind of life pattern has resulted in him being in the front seat and me in the back.

Some people might say that this is natural, since I am as a woman. There is a common notion that women are inclined to be emotional, sensitive, warm, nurturing, and supportive than men. But not all women are like this. I think the key to maintaining good relationships and allyships is to be aware of our differences and manage the tensions that arise from these differences. My husband and I have learned this lesson well in the past seventeen years. What makes our allyship so strong and effective is that we are both cognizant of our differences and use them to complement each other, covering each other's blind spots rather than clashing in disagreements.

Reflection 2 – Women Are Likely to Face Greater Choice Constraints than Men

As a wife and the mother of three growing children, I have found that my choices are always accompanied by constraint. With a family, you do not have the luxury of toying with different options or always opting for your preference. You are tied up with a variety of responsibilities and obligations, including your own well-being and that of your parents, spouse, children, friends, colleagues at work, members of your faith community, other inhabitants of your town or city, etc. You feel responsible to these people because they are important to you and deserve your attention and time. Their happiness is also yours. And these responsibilities and connections are both external and self-imposed.

An example of external obligations, not all of which are positive, are the social norms and practices that predefine women's roles in society. Korean women, for example, are expected to be nurturers and boundary-keepers for their families, so that their husbands can focus on being successful career-wise and their children can grow up to be capable and independent. This boundary-keeping and nurturing are considered womanly responsibilities. I wouldn't deny that I have embraced these roles without much hesitation, hoping to prove to others that I am a fully capable woman. I chose to do it. But adopting these roles came with personal sacrifices; I had to forego some of my own dreams and opportunities to perform them well. And I hope that my two daughters will be able to consider choices beyond the preordained script that Korean society still offers to girls and young women.

Self-imposed responsibilities come with an even stronger sense of obligation. They can center on both ourselves and others. For myself, my aspiration is to tend to my health, spirituality, happiness, self-worth, security, recognition, wealth, achievements, and reputation. No one would deny that these obligations are—and should be—of prime importance to everyone. But others—our families, friends, and colleagues—are also important responsibilities that bind us as individuals. In a way, all of us are tied to one another, existing both for ourselves and to support others. It is our relationships and our commitment to them that define not only our state of mind but our capacities as leaders.

How do we organize our priorities, amid all these obligations? Most of us do not have the time and energy to give everyone in our lives an equal amount of attention and caring. I find my various roles—as wife, mother, daughter and daughter-in-law, pianist, friend, part-time business consultant, and community supporter—consistently taxing and sometimes overwhelming. I can't always keep up with all of my responsibilities. Just being a wife and mother frequently seems like two full-time jobs.

So how should I manage my time so that my integrity and commitment to my responsibilities do not waver? Before my marriage, I didn't make many choices on my own. Then, as a wife, I discovered a lot of tension between self-driven and external responsibilities. Most of the time in our family, priority-setting has been contingent upon my husband's plans and decisions and our children's interests and needs. To keep me going, I have had to step back from my situation, gain a larger perspective, and learn to juggle many competing priorities.

Even with this tightrope work, I realized early on that I would have to abandon some of my most treasured dreams in order to prioritize my family: my careers, a business I managed, even attending one of the world's most renowned music schools, the Berklee College of Music in Boston. These choices were difficult, but rather than feeling discouraged, I tried to reframe my perspective, perceiving the situation as one in which I was preparing for rewards to come.

One of the activities that became most rewarding was developing and nurturing relationships and allyships with the people around me. Wherever I found myself, I was always eager to befriend others, initiate dialogues, share, and learn. I also searched for avenues in which I could attend to some of my high-priority responsibilities, improving both my own life and others'. One of these avenues was serving in our church as a pianist; I have also helped to run the children's choir and undertake a variety of women's outreach activities. I've found these activities both inspiring and deeply satisfying.

Ndileka Mandela, Founder of the Thembekile Mandela Foundation and the first granddaughter of Nelson Mandela, once said, "The biggest challenge for women in the twenty-first century revolves around the issue of choice—the freedom for women to choose who they become." I could not agree more with this statement, and I believe that to achieve this goal women must proactively find and seize the opportunities that they find most meaningful and worthwhile.

Reflection 3 – Women Are As Great As Men, and We Are Showing It Now

Gender stereotypes and the societal perceptions of what men and women should or shouldn't do are, for the most part, more rigid and prevalent in Asia than in the West. There is a deeply rooted patriarchal tradition in Asia. You are considered a "good" woman if you are married and have children and a prosperous husband. If you lack any of these things, people will see you as negligent of your duties, perhaps even lacking in some emotional capacity or having personality issues. Men in Asia also face heavy expectations, but in general Asian societies are more lenient with men than with women.

At the age of twenty-three, I was the executive director of a thriving start-up. I was a successful young businesswoman, yet I was constantly bombarded with questions and comments about my duties as a woman, and about marriage in particular. I felt very uncomfortable in this situation and was shocked by the fact that my community seemed to accept such behavior. More disturbing was the thought that hundreds of millions of women in Asia were experiencing the same bombardment daily. Since then, I have felt a deep conviction that all women should speak up boldly in support of their own desires and independence, and that all men should acknowledge women's rights and speak out themselves on the need for gender equality.

I believe there is a reason why God designed husbands and wives to be partners for life. In every marriage, each partner has strengths and weaknesses, talents and blind spots. Each is created to complement the other. But as far as the capabilities of men and women are concerned, I believe they are equal. I have seen this in all walks of life. I don't believe in "men stuff" or "women's things." Although I agree that women often differ from men in their traits, styles, preferences, and choices—as I said, I have discovered great differences between me and my husband—I also believe that God created men and women to be equals and complements to each other, just as there can be strong partnerships between women and women, and men and men.

I also believe that certain contexts require certain leadership traits, styles, and decisions, whether in men or in women. During the pandemic I have read several articles on women's leadership, including "Why More Countries Need Female Leaders" in US News (March 8, 2021), "Women Are Better Leaders During a Crisis" in the Harvard Business Review (December 30, 2020), and "The Covid Crisis Shows Why We Need More Female Leadership" in Fortune (March 18, 2021). The question raised and discussed in all of these articles was whether women are more qualified than men to lead in times of extreme uncertainty and complexity, such as the current era of the Covid-19 pandemic.

To compress these articles' many points into four key elements: first, looking at female heads of state from Taiwan, New Zealand, Germany, Denmark, Slovakia, and Finland, one can see that these women leaders not only took swift and thorough actions to prevent the spread of Covid-19 but also showed their own vulnerability in order to make connections with their country's populations, genuinely and emotionally, with compassion. Second, these women leaders prioritized human lives above other matters and were more risk-conscious on behalf of their constituencies. Third, these leaders tended to pursue more horizontal, less hierarchical leadership styles in order to get things done; they consistently put the needs of others above their own status and self-interest. Fourth, these leaders placed a huge emphasis on the need for clarity and authenticity in their governments' communications, which translated to better and quicker decision-making.

I was deeply inspired by what I read about these female heads of state. They show by example that women can effectively exercise leadership not only at home but in the workplace and in our communities. But I also believe that their methods are not necessarily superior approaches to leadership. Again, effective leadership must be contextual. Depending on the circumstances, different styles or approaches should be used. At times, leadership focusing on compassion and communication may bring greater value, but in certain settings a more hierarchical, traditionally masculine approach might be more effective. The main point to remember is that such styles are not mutually exclusive. In times like today, with high volatility and ambiguity, we need everyone's leadership style, and our collective awareness of that need will be the game-changer. In other words, being highly cognizant of which leadership style, whether hierarchical, collaborative, or both, is most pertinent in any particular context, will be critical to our survival.

Fundamentally, I believe that both men and women must learn to strike a balance, knowing when to lead and when to support. The more flexible we can become in our roles, the stronger our partnerships and allyships will become, and the more progress and results we will be able to achieve. If we consider our partners and allies—whether they are spouses, colleagues, friends, or even new acquaintances—as God-prepared champions and supporters whom we can both lead and follow, then I believe we will all be able to thrive in this world, no matter how challenging our situation may become.

So What Can We Do to Become Leaders and Allies in Our Own Lives?

This brings me to my last message, a list of the principles that have helped to keep me going in my life despite many challenges and responsibilities. These principles have enabled me to live joyously and meaningfully. Please take them as humble suggestions for your own lives.

1. Identify Your Outlet

I don't like pressures, complexities, and challenges. Even though I am a musician who often has to perform on stage, I have never enjoyed this experience. I become easily overwhelmed when I face constraints and priority conflicts. But this vulnerability has taught me that keeping myself in good spirits and maintaining positive energy are critical for my own survival. I don't have the luxury of running away from my responsibilities, so I have identified several remedies to help me when I feel overwhelmed. These remedies include chatting with my friends, parents, and children; engaging in physical exercise; setting aside two hours of "me time" daily; playing the piano; going shopping; and engaging in prayers.

When I asked my husband what methods he uses to avoid becoming overwhelmed by his responsibilities, he said that he needs tennis every day, teaching, coaching, writing, and traveling, among other precious activities.

These are simple things, but such activities really do make a significant difference. Everyone needs one or more outlets that can release the negative energies built up during the taxing pressures we all encounter daily. Being cognizant of your own state is critical to finding and maintaining such outlets. Asking about other people's outlets may also help you find your own. Together, as men and women, we should all strive to help each other find more creative and effective ways to keep us going.

2. Find Your Allies

As I mentioned earlier, I have lived in many different places around the world. Because of my constant moving, when I was younger, I developed persistent fears and anxiety about building deep relationships with other people. My nomadic life still continues, sadly or luckily depending on how you look at it, but despite these circumstances I have learned to push my own boundaries and start building new relationships whenever I move to a new place.

At this moment, I have been based in Malaysia for the past six years, and I feel deeply blessed by the friends I have made here. When I look closely at these relationships, I can see that they fall into four groups: the parents of kids from our children's school, church friends, common-interest buddies, and confidants who clicked well with me as individuals. All of these groups are important to me and can be found in many other people's lives as well.

Over the years, I have developed robust allyships with these people, and we have become each other's sounding boards. When I feel lost—like the recent time when I heard about my father's diagnosis of a stage-three cancer—or when my husband's long absences leave me lonely and deeply fatigued, my allies are there to lend ears and hands, to resuscitate me emotionally and spiritually, and to inspire me to see the brighter side of myself and the world.

Allies like these are critical in keeping you going and making your life worth living. They are also critical in creating leaders: no one can lead who has no friends and allies. But, as I have mentioned, allyships require commitment, and that commitment must be accompanied by genuine emotion, concern for others, compassion, humanity, and consistency.

3. Anchor Yourself to Your Values and Aspirations

It is important to have a guiding star that shows you where to go when you feel lost. Everyone gets worn out sometimes and feels ill-equipped to face life's daunting responsibilities. We are also all vulnerable to distractions and temptations. However, as long as we know what what's most important to us and our lives, then we can correct our course and keep moving in the right direction. We must constantly engage in candid reality checks and make sure that are actions align with our values—our vision of who we want to become and who we ought to be.

My own values mirror the faith I keep and practice. My Christian faith has taught me the power of a life led by God and the importance of accountability, integrity, compassion, perseverance, optimism, and positivity. These are the core values to which I anchor myself in every aspect of my life.

Equally important are our aspirations. We all have dreams. My children and I talk about our future plans all the time. At this point, I know that my dreams are not as ambitious as my husband's. But having a dream in the first place—even if it's only a short-term plan or hope—is what's important. Such a dream will inspire and excite you, waking you up early in the morning.

My dream has always been to help others through music. My mother started telling me when I was five and first started playing piano that she thanked God for giving me this great gift and prayed that I would use it to help other people thrive. I have been so deeply grateful for the impact I've been able to make through music.

I also try to help others by listening. My friends have told me that they find peace in talking to me. All I ever do is lend my ears to them, pray with and for them, and try to cheer them up, but these humble tools work, and my ambition is to continue these efforts, supporting them through all their challenges. From a grand perspective, such dreams may look vague and modest, but what matters most is having them, and pursuing them for the betterment of yourself and others.

Over the years, many of my women friends have shared stories with me about their relationship challenges, at home and in the workplace. Summing it up, they often conclude that their difficulties stem from choice constraints, conflicts in priority-setting, and other aspects of human dynamics. At such moments, I always remind them of the importance of anchoring yourself to your core values and aspirations.

4. Nudge People to Think and Act for Change

In the systemic challenge of changing social perceptions about women and our roles, we should not shy away from confronting the complexity and difficulty of this task. Both women and men need to make continuous efforts to rewrite preconceived notions about gender, as well as alter traditional gender narratives and practices. We should educate our sons to embrace, respect, and support the immense power and potential that women possess, while educating our daughters to believe that the sky is the only limit to who they can be and what they can achieve.

There is a saying that I particularly like, first spoken by Margaret Mead: "Never doubt that a small group of thoughtful, committed citizens can change the world. Indeed, it is the only thing that ever has." My husband and I have initiated many conversations on this topic with our children. His full-time job is to coach leaders around the globe, helping them to improve our world, and both he and I feel strongly that such work should begin at home.

With our girls especially, we talk at length about the many admirable women leaders out there. We give them articles and op-eds on the lives of such leaders as Ruth Bader Ginsburg, the U.S. Supreme Court Justice; Indra Nooyi, CEO of PepsiCo; Mary Barra, CEO of

GM; Malala Yousafzai, the well-known activist from Pakistan; Angela Merkel, former Chancellor of Germany; Kathrin Jansen, Head of Vaccine R&D at Pfizer; and many others. We encourage our girls to be inspired, excited, and imaginative as they read these stories. In addition, we have made sure to introduce them to our female mentors, friends, and allies, showing them by example the many roles that women can play.

One thing I wouldn't do is spoon-feed or indoctrinate my children with one particular mode of thinking. Rather, by exposing our daughters to a variety of stories and information, I hope that they will think independently, broadly, and deeply on a wide range of issues affecting our world today.

Rectifying the many generalized, inaccurate, or constraining narratives and notions about women all over the globe is a massive systemic challenge. However, if parents, teachers, and influencers all strive to do so using as many avenues as possible, then we will collectively make progress. And, again, this effort should not come solely from women. Just as my husband and I operate as a team in raising our children, so the fight for gender equality must be a joint effort between men and women. As my husband always says, leadership works best when we exercise it in partnership.

We are living in an ever more complex and challenging environment that requires all of us to adapt continuously. This means adopting new perspectives, embracing new ways of doing things, finding new ways of working together, and charting new dreams and directions. Overcoming the systemic challenges placed on women won't be easy, and to succeed we will have to be continuously cognizant of our contexts and our partners. Given these difficulties, let us not forget that men are our close allies, with whom we can reach farther than ever before.

| Chapter 06 |

From Surviving to Thriving:
Moving the Needle on Gender Equality In- and Outside of the Workplace

Mieke Klanker
MA, Science Po Paris
Senior Manager, Deloitte Netherlands

●●●

Panchayat—The Indian Experience

In January 2018, after returning to Amsterdam from the Asia Leadership Trek (ALT)—a study tour and community-service program run by the Center for Asia Leadership—I, together with eight other women, initiated a support circle that we named "Panchayat." This circle was a tight-knit group of working women who joined together to support one another professionally and personally, to forge new opportunities, to build deep connections, and to develop confidence and leadership capabilities. Each of us came from a different background, academically and professionally. I worked in financial services; others came from the realms of journalism, arts and culture, NGOs, legal affairs, public relations, and municipality management.

108 Part 2 Developing Inner Capacities

The name of our circle, Panchayat, is Hindi and refers to a village council comprising five wisemen, acknowledged by the community as its governing body.[1] The inspiration for naming our circle Panchayat came from one of the most moving meetings I attended during the ALT. The Trek had started a month earlier, in December 2017: a group of fifteen graduate students and professionals from more than ten different countries traveled over three weeks through five countries in Asia—Malaysia, India, Singapore, Korea, and Japan. Engaging with leaders in government, business, and the non-profit sector, we learned a lot about the political, economic, industrial, and societal issues facing each of these countries. In India alone, we visited four cities—New Delhi, the nation's political capital; Mumbai, its business capital; Nagpur; and the village of Anji in central India.

India is a country very close to my heart, as I worked there for three years between earning my Bachelor's and Master's degrees. As a 21-year-old, I embarked on an adventure that transformed me into an independent and resilient adult. I learned how to deal with many novel situations in a completely unfamiliar environment, and the experience gave me countless great memories.

In India, the Panchayat village councils settle disputes between individuals and among villages, a practice that dates back to 250 CE. In Anji, we learned that the villagers there have transformed this practice into a modern structure, enabling all of them, women and men, young and old, to share their struggles and experiences by creating their own panchayats for different peer groups—just like my peer group in Amsterdam. The villagers told us how they provided support to each other in life's ups and downs by creating a safe environment in their panchayats. Most impressively, the women described how they had sought access to micro-loans, initiated small agro-businesses,

---

1   www.merriam-webster.com/dictionary/panchayat.

sold and reaped their businesses' returns to scale, and provided a living for their families and communities by offering employment. Their experiences dismantled prevalent perceptions about what women can and cannot do in their community. The men, in turn, told us how their spouses' success had transformed their lives, and how they had partnered with them to support and nurture their businesses.

We also learned how the panchayats had transformed some women from victims of domestic violence and poverty into successful achievers of their aspirations. These stories blew my mind. At first sight, there seemed to be many contrasts between the villagers and us ALT participants—in the way we looked, dressed, spoke, and thought. However, thanks to the safe spaces that the villagers had created in their panchayats, we were able to exchange insights and best practices, mutually testing our assumptions. The eagerness to connect was palpable and reached beyond our cultural and language differences.

The honesty and openness with which the women of Anji shared what they had learned from each other made a deep and lasting impression on me, so much so that I proposed "Panchayat" as the name of our new circle in Amsterdam after my return from the ALT. The circle led to my first experience of linking leadership with Inclusion & Diversity (I&D), a connection that would play a larger role in the next years of my life. In this chapter, I would like to take you along in my experiences and share my lessons learned.

Panchayat: The Netherlands Experience

After witnessing the impact of the panchayat on the women in Anji, I viewed our Panchayat in Amsterdam as symbolizing the strength and optimism I had found there—the feeling of being surrounded and backed by a group of women, sharing and learning from each other's experiences and perspectives, and being each other's champions. This was the kind of space that we aspired to create with our circle in the Netherlands. The eight of us agreed to meet once every two months, on a Sunday afternoon. Among other activities, we invited women role-models to share their experiences and insights with us; hosted workshops on personal branding, pitching yourself, and managing personal finances; organized sessions on yoga and meditation; and shared voting strategies to increase women's representation in the local elections.

We often had so much to share about our lives that we had to keep our real catch-up until after the "official" activities of each meeting. By sharing the intimate happenings of our lives over the years, we became each other's close supporters and confidantes. Over time, some of our Panchayat members left, while new ones joined our circle; some of us became mothers, went on world trips, changed careers, or had to deal with health issues. In all of these circumstances, we could reach out to and count on each other, whether for a connection to a good employment lawyer, support when a relationship broke down, or advice on how to make a career move.

Our Dutch version of the Panchayat was also inspired by my reading of Sheryl Sandberg's book Lean In: *Women, Work and the Will to Lead*, which calls for women in the workplace to organize themselves in circles that will support their ambitions. The book was intended to address the challenges women face when advancing their career, and it taught me some important lessons from a senior woman who had steadily climbed the career ladder, or "jungle gym," as she calls it. According to Sandberg, when you are a working woman, you can climb multiple ways to reach the top—just like being in a jungle gym. Being freed from the stress of having to pursue one route allows you to be creative in your approaches, allowing you to stay calmer and happier, while perhaps advancing even more quickly.

Another thing the book taught me was that, as women, we are sometimes held to different standards than men. As a woman you are often expected to be nice and feminine, to avoid coming across as rude, and to argue for what you want without coming across too aggressively. Meeting these expectations can require advanced verbal and behavioral acrobatics, as I have experienced myself several times. For instance, when I shared with a superior that I felt ready for the next promotion round, I was told that I was expressing myself too assertively.

By the end of 2018, our Panchayat had connected with several other circles in the Netherlands, and together we established the Lean In Netherlands chapter of LeanIn.org, a global non-profit organization designed "to offer women the ongoing inspiration and support to help them achieve their goals, and offer educational resources and programming that encourages women's leadership."[2] By early 2019, we had established a foundation to achieve three key initiatives. First, we aimed to increase women's professional capacity-building and personal leadership in our community, through the establishment of additional circles and the increase of support to existing circles. Second, we aimed to bring together circles across the country by organizing events, connecting female movers-and-shakers, and mobilizing more people to advocate for gender equality. Third, we hosted unconscious-bias workshops and campaigns based on the "50 Ways to Fight Bias" materials of LeanIn.org. These workshops focused on common biases that women face in the workplace, with the aim of empowering all employees to identify and challenge bias head-on.

By volunteering to be the Treasurer of Lean In Netherlands, I put my professional expertise to use for a cause close to my heart.

---

2   leanin.org

After ten months, I was asked to join the foundation's Board, and by mid-2021, as the Chair of the Board, I was heading an organization comprising 35 volunteers. Within that timeframe, we had created and connected with 30 active circles, moved our face-to-face meetings to virtual events that reached an audience beyond the Netherlands, and hosted many events and panels on topics such as personal finance, well-being, and negotiation skills. In 2021, we organized over twenty "50 Ways to Fight Bias" workshops for a diverse group of organizations, engaging with and educating over 15 participants per training session on unconscious bias. We built a large community of followers on social-media channels, and—last but certainly not least—we inspired and enabled numerous people to start circles for themselves.

Systemic Challenges in the Netherlands

The Netherlands is a high-income, wealthy and socially and politically stable country, where women rarely encounter the daunting challenges that women in other countries often face. When it comes to gender equality, the Netherlands ranks 31st out of 156 countries on the World Economic Forum's 2021 Global Gender Gap Report—ahead of several other European countries, including Luxembourg, Italy, and Greece, though significantly below the Nordic countries of Iceland, Finland, and Norway, as well as below Rwanda, Nicaragua, the Philippines, and Serbia. In the Netherlands, we pride ourselves on providing equal opportunities to everyone, with close to 100% of children enrolled in primary education and more women than men enrolled in tertiary education (90.9% versus 79.3%).[3]

---

3   www.weforum.org/reports/global-gender-gap-report-2021.

However, the gender gap in our country is persistent, and is especially visible in senior and managerial positions in the private and public sectors. The limited presence of women in senior leadership roles shows that a "glass ceiling" is still in place, with women holding only 27% of senior and managerial positions.[4] In a dramatic illustration of this imbalance, in 2022 there were more CEOs named Peter (a common male name in the Netherlands) than there were women holding that position. When it comes to politics, the Netherlands has never had a woman serve as the head of state (the Prime Minister), and over the last decades women's representation in the government's cabinet has fluctuated between 25 and 30 percent.[5]

Prime Minister Mark Rutte commented on the limited number of women in his cabinet in 2017 by saying, "My aim is to find the best people; the male/female distribution is secondary."[6] He implied with this comment that there were no qualified women available. However, the new government that formed in January 2022, led by the same Prime Minister, has equal representation of men and women in the cabinet and also boasts the first ever women to lead the influential Ministry of Finance and the Ministry of Social Affairs. So, although there is still a world to win, we have seen good progress in terms of women's representation in politics. The business world will hopefully soon follow suit, pushed by a law enacted in September 2021 that requires a more balanced ratio between men and women in management and supervisory boards.[7]

As stated earlier, more women than men enroll in tertiary education in the Netherlands, but women are not only underrepresented in the higher echelons of the labor market, they are underrepresented

---

4   www.brandedu.nl/mijnnaamispeter/#toggle-id-1.
5   www.fd.nl/politiek/1425537/rutte-iv-breekt-records-vooral-met-de-inbreng-van-vrouwen.
6   www.ad.nl/politiek/rutte-verdeling-man-vrouw-in-kabinet-is-bijzaak-a42b6713/.
7   www.eerstekamer.nl/nieuws/20210928/eerste_kamer_steunt_evenwichtiger.

across the labor market as a whole. Experts often argue that this is due to 60% of Dutch women working only part-time (i.e. working between 12 and 36 hours per week; 35-40 hours is considered full-time in the Netherlands)—this is roughly three times the OECD average of women working part-time and over three times the percentage of Dutch men working part-time.[8] While it is beneficial for society for women to be active participants in the labor market, their mostly part-time roles contribute to a continued gender gap in earnings and pensions, women's slower progression into management roles, and the unequal division of unpaid work at home.[9]

These gaps typically widen with parenthood, as mothers often reduce their working hours to take on more of the unpaid care work at home. After becoming a mother, 40% of women in the Netherlands reduce their working hours or cease going to work completely, whereas men continue to work the same number of hours. Although Dutch society accepts men caring for their children and women having jobs, it continues to expect women to prioritize their families over their work, whereas men are expected to favor their careers over their families.[10] These expectations are often explicitly stated by family or friends, as well as being implied by more subtle behaviors, such as mothers being on first call at children's daycare centers instead of fathers.

Creating awareness of these patterns and openness in discussing them among family, friends, and colleagues are the first steps toward encouraging everyone to make more conscious choices about life and work, and eventually coming closer to equality between men and

---

8   www.oecd.org/social/part-time-and-partly-equal-gender-and-work-in-the-netherlands
9   Dutch women spend on average 27 hours per week on care and household tasks, while men spend only about 17 hours per week.
10   www.nrc.nl/nieuws/2021/09/20/fulltime-werken-en-parttime-moederen-waarom-doen-zo-weinig-vrouwen-dat-a4058926.

women. For the Netherlands, improving women's participation in the labor market and advancing their economic empowerment are important elements in building diverse, inclusive, and innovative organizations and a more equal society overall. It would also result in a projected economic benefit of €10.8 billion additional GDP according to research by Dutch bank ABN AMRO.[11]

Even if the Netherlands is advancing in terms of gender equality, common biases against women persist. For instance, a likeability bias affects women holding powerful positions in the public eye; they come under more scrutiny than their male counterparts, as could be seen vividly when Femke Halsema's position as the first female Mayor of Amsterdam was questioned because of her family circumstances and when Sigrid Kaag, the first female leader of the liberal political party D66, spoke out about her ambition to become Prime Minister. Both women drew a lot of attention due to their circumstances and ambitions, and endured a public backlash in which their tones of voice and behaviors were described as "difficult" or "arrogant."

A Call to Action

This broader picture of gender inequality in the Netherlands is reflected in explicit and subtle challenges that Dutch women, including myself and my female friends, face on a day-to-day basis. Such challenges were part of what motivated me to become an active volunteer for Lean In Netherlands, and I am eager to share the insights and lessons I have gained from these experiences, as well my experiences in the workplace, which hopefully will inspire the readers of this book.

---

11 https://www.abnamro.com/nl/nieuws/gelijke-verdeling-on-betaald-werk-goed-voor-1000-euro-extra-per-huishouden

1. Be an Inclusion & Diversity (I&D) Changemaker

For over ten years, I have been a consultant in Mergers & Acquisitions (M&A), working in different countries across the world and periodically moving to new fields of expertise. Broadening my horizons has kept me energized. The consultancy field in which I work is a male-dominated environment, and so are many of the client teams we interact with, both on the Board level and in the Finance and Operations Departments.

While I was in the junior ranks, gender in our team was strongly tilted toward men (70/30), and in the senior ranks there were no women at all. It was clear that women were not the norm in the industry. For instance, when a more senior woman joined, I was told by the partner, "We now also have a lady in the team who wears heels and dresses—that's something new for the boys, they have to get used to it." A few years later, an internal analysis showed that, across the ranks, women on average took a year longer to get promoted to the next level than men did. Did this indicate that the women were less apt for their roles or was it due to certain so-called "masculine characteristics" being favored by the people in charge of promotions (mostly men)? In my work environment, being confident, decisive, and competitive was valued. Yet , as a woman, speaking out or being assertive, I was sometimes criticized for being "dominant" or "angry." It felt like walking on a tightrope.

A few years ago, the photo for my office team's chat group was changed to a picture of our team on a boat during our most recent team event. Although I had been aware of the limited number of women in my work environment, this picture made it strikingly obvious: I was confronted by the fact that I was the only woman in a group of more than 25 people. The two other women in the team had not been able to attend the event, and so, during this team get-away, I had felt alone, especially after several colleagues pointed out that I would be the only woman staying overnight. The photo on the boat made me feel deeply uneasy, for it clearly showed the lack of gender diversity on the team. The result was that I decided to become active as an I&D ambassador at work.

I am part of a group of 150 people working in M&A. For the I&D initiative, we created a small team of five colleagues and initiated several conversations about I&D in the larger group. We sent out a survey to gain a better understanding of the key challenges and issues involving I&D in our wider team, and we then translated the results into infographics, realizing that communicating on this topic in the way the M&A team was used to, with numbers and hard facts, was the best way to get our message across. Next, we analyzed the main topics identified by our colleagues and collected the most honest and thought-provoking comments from the survey as talking points. Finally, we organized I&D sessions for groups of up to 10 people to talk about everyone's experiences, based on the graphs and comments from the survey.

In a work environment where people are valued by the number of hours they spend on client work, the tricky part in our initiative was to claim space and time. After gaining support from our senior leadership for our approach, we created time in everyone's agenda—and, just as importantly, in our own agendas—to run these sessions. The meetings were engaging, with open and illuminating discussions on the topics that emerged from the survey. People shared personal experiences and learned more about each other, and, through the conversations, everyone realized that our team was more diverse than they had anticipated. The discussions covered topics very different from those normally discussed between colleagues, such as the environments they had grown up in or how they balanced their family life at home with their work life. Crucial for the success of these sessions was the active participation—and vulnerability—of members of our senior leadership in each session.

After we had successfully hosted the sessions, the leadership team of our department invited us to present our outcomes. At this point, we realized that our main achievement was not so much unveiling new insights but more so simply initiating discussions and keeping the momentum going with conversations about inclusion, diversity, and people's personal experiences and feelings. Again, to make our effort concrete, we framed our achievement in terms of hours spent: through the sessions we realized a total of 150 I&D-impact hours (150 people for 1 hour).

Although in the process I sometimes encountered resistance and at times even felt like an activist in the workplace, I realized that I was applying different skills from those I used in my regular job, and that being active on topics like these can attract executive management interest and exposure.

From the time when I first began my career in M&A, a lot has changed: I&D is now a topic high on the agenda across the industry. In the junior ranks, the women/men ratio has become 50/50, with greater female representation also appearing in the senior ranks. In fact, our department of 600 people is now led by a woman. Although all this is an impressive change in the last ten years, it doesn't mean that we can now rest on our laurels; it is crucial that we maintain diversity and ensure that our workplace is inclusive, allowing everyone to feel that they can be themselves. This should be our continuous effort and point of focus.

2. Show Up and Speak Up

Even before formally taking the initiative on I&D at work, I tended to be vocal on this topic. In one instance, I responded publicly to a male colleague who suggested that a female colleague had been hired not because of her capabilities but because of her physical appearance. I expressed my concern about this comment's relevance and appropriateness—but, as I spoke, I felt very lonely and vulnerable because none of the men or women in the room backed me up. Some of my male colleagues even lamented, "Oh, now that there are women in the team, we can no longer make these types of remarks anymore."

Some years later, two of my colleagues told me that they still remembered this incident. They thanked me and said they were glad that I had addressed the colleague's inappropriate remark. I learned then that they had been silently agreeing with me when I spoke out. It was a relief, though I also asked why they hadn't expressed their support on the spot, as it would have made a tremendous difference to me. Their validation, even though it came years later, strengthened my belief that we shouldn't shy away from voicing our feelings and thoughts. In a later performance review, I was lauded for my behavior—my seniors recognized that my effort to challenge the status quo had brought others to change their perspectives. So, although feeling alone in the moment, I eventually gained support and recognition for my action.

Throughout the past several years, I have benefited from the strong external support of the powerful women at Lean In, which empowered me to lead the change in my workplace. In the Lean In environment, discussing gender inequality is normal, and we often talk about signs of inequality in our professional environments. Being part of this community has strengthened me and enabled me to advocate equality in my workplace; it has consistently given me strength when overcoming adversity, being challenged by colleagues who question the relevance of diverse teams, keeping up the energy level of our I&D team, and seeking new perspectives on our goals and successes.

3. Diversity Is About Being Yourself

Earlier in my career, I experienced a lack of diversity in my workplace and did not always feel at home. Working in M&A, I was surrounded by men with similar profiles: most of them had graduated from the same universities, were members of the same fraternities, and had studied finance, business, or economics. My colleagues bonded over chats about football and cars, which were far from my favorite pastimes. As an introverted woman with a background in anthropology and international political economy, I sometimes felt out of place. Moreover, I realized that there was no obvious diversity in the cultures or ethnicities represented in my work environment. I was vividly confronted by this homogeneity when mentoring a university student as part of a corporate social responsibility project run by my employer. The student came from a Lebanese background and told me that she was not keen to work for our organization because of the lack of diversity in general, and, more specifically, of people similar to herself.

This student was pointing out the lack of role models for herself in the organization, and I have experienced such moments several times myself. When leading a workshop for a client organization alongside two of their senior female leaders, I mentioned afterward how special it was for me to run the workshop with two other women. They told me that for them the experience was nothing extraordinary, given the more diverse nature of their organization and their industry. Later, when I developed a mentoring relationship with a female partner in our firm, I realized she was the first senior woman I had become close with in my working life thus far. As I listened to her perspective, learned that we had lived through some of the same experiences, and benefited from her advice, I realized that having role models is crucial for our success and well-being. When you discover that there are other people like you, it is easier to be yourself—confidently and openly.

Several times in my career, when singled out as a woman, I have felt that I needed to adjust or learn certain types of behavior to "overcome" certain 'feminine' characteristics. For instance, I once attended a training program for women in management that included recommendations on how to be "accepted" by the (mostly) men around us. We were told that it is preferred to wear our hair in an updo, as it would look more professional than wearing our hair loose. As part of this training we also learned how to present our achievements in a natural way, as women often 'show off' less or tend to think their successes are recognized and appreciated by others naturally, without having been emphasized to them.

These training sessions made me wonder whether women should change their behavior or whether the work environment should change to accommodate women (and, for that matter, all those who do not fit the standard). The latter is what my ideal world would look like, though I acknowledge that, in order to be successful and get results, being flexible and adapting your behavior to different circumstances and people can make you more efficient. From an organizational perspective, management experts have made it clear that increasing diversity does not in itself increase the effectiveness of an organization; what matters is how the organization harnesses that diversity and whether it's willing to change its power structure and corporate culture.[12] These changes necessitate embracing a variety of styles and voices within the organization and less so aiming to train and mold those that have differing styles and voices to conform to the organization's norms, as I have experienced at times.

For me, as I struggled to overcome the challenges of being a woman in a male-dominated workplace, the women I connected with

---

12 www.hbr.org/2020/11/getting-serious-about-diversity-enough-already-with-business-case.

in my Panchayat circle and through the Lean In network made all the difference. We were role models for each other, proving that our behavior was not flawed, just different from the male status quo.

4. Lift Each Other Up

A few years into my consulting career, I learned that the women in my organization were compared to each other in our performance reviews: I, for example, was told at some point that I was "the best among the women." Apparently, my boss was putting his employees into two different boxes, the men and the women. I wondered why I could not be compared with everyone around me, regardless of gender. However, I also realized that I myself sometimes felt more competitive toward the other women in my workplace than toward the men. Given that we women made up only a handful of the group as a whole, it sometimes felt as if we had to compete for a limited number of spots.

In hindsight, I view this attitude as conforming to the "queen bee" style of behavior toward female colleagues. This is something we can avoid and counter by supporting each other and by sharing experiences, as I eventually did with two female colleagues. We created a safe space where we could swap stories about our male-dominated work environment and make jokes about it. These positives connections were far more valuable to me than my previous competitive attitude, and made me realize how important it is for women to support, uplift, and celebrate each other. My two female colleagues are still my go-to advisors on many topics related to the workplace, and we share our experiences over dinner once every quarter. Congratulating each other on our successes brings us closer together and takes each of us further. For all of us, bringing such support actively into practice not only empowers the people we celebrate but shines a light on ourselves.

5. Create Your Own Opportunities

My last pieces of advice are to express your ambitions to those around you, say yes to growth opportunities, create these opportunities yourselves, and work in fields that you feel passionate about. For me, those fields have been exposure to different cultures, I&D, and sustainability. I have blended each of these areas into my work experience, and they have enriched me on a personal level too.

After working and living in India for three years, I was keen to enjoy similarly enriching international experiences as a consultant. So, when the opportunity came, I expressed to my seniors my ambition to build on my international experience. This resulted in two extended periods of working outside the Netherlands—in Vienna, Austria, and in Istanbul, Turkey. These experiences provided me with inspiring and fresh perspectives. In Austria, though I worked in an all-male team, my colleagues' cultural backgrounds varied from Belgian and Mexican to Brazilian and Swedish. In Turkey, several of the senior positions were held by women, and I learned that it is considered more natural for Turkish women to work full-time and to blend work with family than it is in the Netherlands.

At Lean In Netherlands, all of us share the same passion; we are all volunteers, offering our free time to work toward common goals: gender equality and a new definition of leadership. This effort has given me a different type of fulfilment from what I experience in the workplace. A lot of time and effort are needed to run a foundation of volunteers, though that is more than compensated by the adrenaline and energy generated in every Lean In Netherlands meeting. Hearing from circle members about how the group has positively influenced both their work experiences and their lives—witnessing the direct impact of our efforts on other people—gives me a tremendous feeling of satisfaction and achievement.

Sometimes you may come across opportunities that you do not

yet feel ready to take on. For me, that moment came when I was asked to become a Board member for Lean In Netherlands. I was flattered, but I did not feel prepared or capable enough to lead the foundation. I accepted the position only after I had spoken with one of the existing Board members, who clearly expressed to me that I would have not been asked to take on the role if the Board had not believed that I was the best candidate. This showed me that, often, we are worthy and capable of carrying out a role or task even if it seems daunting at first sight.

Closing Out

Writing this chapter has enabled me to share my experiences and insights with a wider audience; I hope that it will serve as an inspiration for other people to go after their goals and follow their hearts. Remember that achieving a diverse, inclusive, and equal environment is not a challenge to be met solely by those disadvantaged by inequality—whether that is based on gender, sexual preference, cultural backgrounds, or however you frame diversity in your situation or environment. Rather, achieving true equality is also dependent on leadership and the larger group. It is everyone's responsibility to learn how to listen to others' perspectives, refrain from judgement, and solicit feedback on how their behaviors and practices might impede a culture that supports learning, equality, and mutual respect.

The next step for me is to focus on my new role of incorporating sustainability considerations into decision-making within M&A and investments. Overcoming I&D challenges was a lot more fun and a lot easier because I had a tribe of like-minded people around me. Learning from this, I have started to connect with people in my network who focus on sustainability. As I hear their experiences and share my own perspectives, I aim to create another group of like-minded peers and supporters—another circle, in effect—to turn to for advice while diving into this new challenge.

| Chapter 07 |

The Experiences of Four Women Providing Leadership

at International Schools in Southeast Asia

Rebecca Stroud Stasel

Adjunct Assistant Professor

Faculty of Education, Queen's University

●●●

International education has been a burgeoning field for several decades, and with its numerous intricacies and connections to globalization, the field is likely to continue expanding. In their literature review of international education, Dolby and Rahman (2008) parsed this field into six subfields, one of which is international schools. This subfield is perhaps the least represented in empirical studies, especially those that pertain to the lived experiences of teachers and leaders in international schools, and there is, moreover, almost no literature addressing experiences pertaining to gender. This chapter shares a findings from a study on the experiences of sojourning educators at international schools, focusing on some leadership opportunities and challenges experienced by four women working at four different international schools located in Malaysia, Singapore, and Thailand.

International schools have been associated with globalization for centuries. Historically, the shifts in international schooling can be loosely correlated with three eras. The first started with the initial discussions of internationalizing schools, beginning in the 1700s, and sparked a lively debate that is still ongoing today about concepts of peace education (Heater, 2002), international-mindedness, and what it means to be a global citizen (Hill, 2015). This phase lasted through the Hague Peace Conference in 1899 and the creation of the League of Nations in 1921.

The second phase of international schooling saw significant growth following the founding of the United Nations Educational, Scientific, and Cultural Organization (UNESCO) in 1946. Since its inception, UNESCO has dramatically influenced the internationalization of education (White, 2011), frequently engaging in dialogues about the concept of international-mindedness, which can be simply defined as developing pedagogies that promote peace and harmony between cultures (Hill, 2015). It is important to note that some scholars have interrogated the conceptual framing of international-mindedness (e.g., Brown & Lauder, 2001; Haywood, 2015; Tarc, 2013), arguing that the construct has reflected and continues to reflect an Anglo-Western gaze, thus benefitting only targeted political and business interests. This argument leads us to the challenge of defining the concept in a transculturally acceptable way, and then developing ways to promote it more inclusively.

The third stage of international schooling may be understood as a product of globalization and increased global mobility among an increasing number of student stakeholders. The shift followed the creation of the International Baccalaureate Organization (IBO, or IB) in 1968. An explosive growth of international schools ensued, along with a shift in student stakeholder groups. As a result, international schooling has moved away from institutions designed to serve the children of expatriate parents and has focused more on serving the children of growing affluent classes within host countries. This trend has been fed by a popular view of English as the global lingua franca and that international schools offer increased access to elite institutions of higher education, which in turn expands higher-education study opportunities and, by extension, professional opportunities. Recent years have also seen a proliferation of for-profit international schools, which will further change the landscape of international schooling.

The term "international schools" is a contested one, both in scholarship and in practice. Over time, these schools have served a variety of objectives and usages. For the purposes of this chapter, an international school is defined as a predominantly English-language, private, K-12 school that is externally accredited by metrics not created by its host country. International schools are not considered higher education, although they may be linked to or housed on the campuses of higher-education hubs. The schools often serve as gateways to higher education, both within and outside of the host country, and have generally been viewed as offering improved access to higher-education programs in Anglo-Western countries, including the UK, the USA, Canada, Australia, and New Zealand.

As mentioned earlier, the profile of students at international schools has shifted in the past several decades. In the first two stages of international schooling, students in international schools were predominantly children of expatriate parents living and working overseas. However, with the rise of the IB and the changing economies of many countries, especially in the Middle East and South and East Asia, international schools and their focus on global competencies have become increasingly popular among upwardly mobile families within the host countries, who view international schools as facilitating access to higher-education options on a global scale. Accordingly, international-school programs have adapted to serve local student stakeholder groups. Keeling (as cited in PIE News,

2013), observed that "local children fill 80% of international school places, a complete reversal of thirty years ago, when 80% were filled by expatriate children." Keeling further noted that these local children represent the top 5% socioeconomic demographic of their countries. As with the shifts in international-school structures, these demographic shifts are sure to alter stakeholder demands.

Another changing landscape is the profile of the expatriate teacher and leader. Since the inception of international schools, male Anglo-western educators have been the preferred group (Gardner-McTaggart, 2018), and as a result international schools have had the reputation of being "white boys' clubs." This perception is slowly changing. There have been only a few studies analyzing international teaching and school leadership through a gender lens; those that do exist show that men dominate leadership and senior management in international schools. Thearle (1999), found that over half of the staff in international schools were women, but that their representation dropped to 20% for the leadership positions of heads and directors. A more recent study by Sanderson & Whitehead (2016) found that only 25% of the leadership in the international schools studied was female, while over 75% of the teaching force was female (see also PIE News, 2013). This imbalance has also been found in Western public schooling (Whitehead & Moodley, 1999), and thus it may be presumed that the framing of leadership in education generally has been the result of a predominantly male gaze.

These complex and shifting gender dynamics create leadership tensions for all stakeholder groups within international schools, including the school's leaders. This chapter, as noted above, explores the experiences of four women leaders at international schools.

The Gender Gap in Educational Leadership

Education as a profession has long been perceived to be dominated by women, and indeed the majority of K-12 teachers are women. This chapter argues that teachers are leaders (Harris, 2005), who meet diversified and distributed leadership needs within their schools, and that educators in formal leadership positions (e.g., school principals) cannot meet those needs on their own. However, while women teachers make up the majority of the teacher workforce, they continue to be the minority in formal leadership positions within the global education system, thus demonstrating a glass ceiling in education.

In addition to the barriers and challenges facing women in educational fields, there are a variety of challenges facing sojourning educators who work at international schools overseas. Ward et al. (2005, p. 6) defined such sojourners as "between-society culture travelers," and the phenomenon of living between societies has led to theories about borderlands (Anzaldúa, 1987), walking in two worlds (Fitzgerald, 2006), and third-culture kids (Pollock & Van Reken, 2009). An area of common ground among these three theoretical perspectives is the need for individuals in such situations to learn how to adapt quickly. Safdar and Berno (2016) categorized sojourners as "temporary acculturating groups." Acculturation is a two-way process: being influenced by living in a culture other than one's own, and having an influence upon the culture in which one lives (Sam & Berry, 2016). It is also a dynamic process, affected by individual factors, and can take a long time to navigate.

Further impacting international educators' acculturation experiences is the fact that teachers and formal leaders in international schools carry the responsibility of caring for their students, some of whom are also sojourning. Emotional intelligence is thus necessary for effective leadership within these schools (George, 2000). Given that the role of nurturing has long been associated with female professionals more than with their male colleagues, more studies on women educators in international schools are needed, to explore both the complexities that face sojourning teachers and the best methods of supporting sojourning students.

The Study

This chapter follows the experiences of four female sojourning educators, for a period of one and a half years. Each educator was working in one of the four international schools located in Malaysia, Singapore, and Thailand. These four women represent a spectrum of teaching and leadership experiences. One was a head of school, two were teachers with additional positions of responsibility assigned to them, and one was a relatively new teacher who came to the school as an early-career teacher (ECT, a term referring to the first five years of teaching experience) and had just passed this stage at the time of our first interview.

The study was a narrative inquiry (Clandinin, 2013), focusing on the lived experiences of the participants in order to learn from their stories. A variety of data instruments were used; this chapter will share the findings from one-one interviews with the four participants. The four women were initially interviewed using a protocol of seven semi-structured questions and a final open-ended one. Following a prolonged, reflective data-collection phase, the participants were then invited for follow-up one:one interviews.

Participants

Cursory profiles of the four participants are provided below, ordered from least to most leadership experience (including distributed teacher leadership and formal leadership roles). The names of the four participants are pseudonyms.

Hayley: Hayley had not taught in her home country; instead, she chose to sojourn as soon as she graduated from her teacher-preparation program. She spent two years in another country before accepting a teaching position in Malaysia, where she had completed her first contract and was on a contract-renewal position at the time when we first met. Hayley was interested in developing her cultural competencies and selected this area for her leadership development, via opportunities at the school as well as self-directed professional development that included enrolling in a part-time graduate degree program.

Bria: Bria worked as an artist and comedian in her home country prior to moving overseas. Her first overseas teaching position was as an uncertified teacher. She enjoyed this job enough to take a respite from sojourning to obtain teaching certification, and then returned to become a sojourner in Singapore. Bria was drawn to school leadership; she appreciated strong school-community dynamics and believed herself to be competent enough to lead and support a thriving school community. Her leadership capacity was quickly noticed by the school's leadership team, who invited her to take on added responsibilities. At the time of our first meeting, she was the head of her school's primary division, as well as an instructional coach and the director of the theater at the school.

Rowan: Rowan worked as a teacher for a number of years in her home country and took several leaves of absence to sojourn overseas. At the time of our first meeting, she was living and working in Malaysia, on her fourth sojourn. One of her earlier sojourns had been cut short due to a natural disaster that had destroyed the school where she worked. In her current school, Rowan was hired as a guidance coun-sellor—a full-time position that included leadership and outreach. Upon her arrival in host country, further teaching assignments were added to her timetable, which she fulfilled alongside her guidance work.

Jayna: Jayna worked as a teacher for a few years in her home country before taking up an overseas teaching opportunity in another English-speaking country. She ended up living and teaching in three English-speaking countries before sojourning in non-Anglo coun-tries. Over time, Jayna was hired to take on additional responsibilities and soon became a full-time leader as head of primary divisions/schools. At the time of our first interview, she was the principal of a primary school. By the time of our second interview, she was about to accept a position as the director of another international school in another country.

Findings

The findings in this chapter are divided into two categories: "Opportunities" and "Challenges." The examples provided in each from the experiences of the four participants, and may at times give the impression that their experiences were predominantly negative or positive. They were not; all four participants spoke of experiencing both rich opportunities and significant challenges.

A. Opportunities

All women in this study gravitated toward leadership opportuni-ties. Hayley, who moved to Malaysia as an early-career teacher after an earlier and shorter sojourn in another country, found that the school was interested in her leadership capacities, and that she was able to take on added responsibilities at her school in several ways. One involved creating a mentorship program, which paired newly hired teachers with seasoned teachers in the same department, so as to give them curricular and departmental support. Hayley explained: "I was part of this initiative. We created a new staff committee, and this committee is in charge of having teacher mentors for each of the new staff, that they can go to. [...] We first ask the current staff for volunteers, and then we select the volunteers based on their subject area. We try to pair someone that is teaching at least in the same department [...], like [a] math teacher with a math teacher; obviously they could hopefully help them with the content if they have questions about that as well."

Many schools, both international and local, use similarly conceived mentorship programs. However, Hayley said that the program she helped to develop specifically focused on the acculturation of newly hired staff. She described the need for mentors to be flexible and able to give support in a number of areas: "But also being someone who is approachable to talk to you about anything. Like, 'Hey, I don't know where to go buy my groceries,' or 'I don't know how to get to the clinic. Can you show me where it is?' Of course, around the school, I show them where things are and help them in that way. But also, on a personal note, we've found that it's been quite successful. I think the new staff seemed very, very happy, and they've acclimatized a lot better, I think."

While developing the program, Hayley learned about acculturative challenges experienced by other staff-members, and the ways in which these challenges intersected with organizational behaviors. She observed: "[T]he staffs from the previous semester, we found out, had a lot of problems acclimatizing because they all came in at different times. There were issues with visas. [...] Normally what happens is all the new staff will arrive within a few days of each other, and they have a lot of time to bond. And that bonding I think helps them to lessen the culture shock."

Hayley began teaching internationally as soon as she graduated-from her teachers' preparation program in Canada, at a time when local teaching jobs were hard to find. Rather than spending several years as an occasional (substitute) teacher who would not have access to the capacity-building professional opportunities that full-time teachers enjoyed, she went overseas, where she was able to begin in a position that encompassed more responsibility. When she arrived in Malaysia, the leaders at her school were enthusiastic about her leader-ship ideas. She believed that developing cultural competencies would strengthen her teaching, especially when working with a transnational student body, and set targeted professional-development goals for herself. At the time of our meeting, Hayley was also pursuing an advanced degree virtually, with a focus on cultural competencies in the classroom.

In contrast with Hayley, Bria found her career as a teacher by happenstance, having worked in the arts and as a comedian first. She discussed the challenges of acculturation and described feeling compelled to project optimism and energy in order to contribute to the positive working morale in her school. Her optimism was soon noticed by the school's leadership team, and she was offered leader-ship opportunities of her own, becoming an instructional coach, a theater director, and eventually a member of the leadership team itself. She was even encouraged to consider becoming a principal. However, while Bria loved to lead and felt that it was an innate part of her being, she was concerned that being a principal might limit both her professional diversity and her art-making opportunities. She was content to thrive as a lead teacher and instructional coach, center-ing her work around compassion coupled with high standards. This approach became invaluable at the onset of the pandemic, during which she generated numerous lessons in video format and provided expertise and modeling for other teachers at the school.

At one point, Bria was asked to pinpoint the type of leader she wanted to become. In her words, the leadership team asked her, "'Do you want to be the kind of teacher who teaches students, the kind of teacher who teaches teachers, or the kind of teacher who influences policy?' And I said, 'all three.'" She has continued to work toward each of these goals. Conceptualizing her form of leadership, she explained, "It makes me feel good to make others feel good too. [...] Leadership also relies on your human connection with others. [...] Typically, I reach out, I'm always the person to reach out. [...] You have to leave room for also just that human connection, connecting with people."

Jayna also emphasized the importance of human connection, and argued that women leaders provide critical nurturing in both primary schools, and secondary schools: "The reason why women are good [leaders and] ahead of priorities [is] because we actually care. [...] I've visited quite a few schools. I think that secondary schools could learn a lot from the primary, especially [in areas] like transition[s] and dealing with issues that children have."

B. Challenges

Jayna self-identified as a global nomad (McCaig, 2002), a career international teacher, and a leader. She began her sojourning at schools in Anglo-Western countries, which she believed made it easier for her to adapt to other cultures later. She enjoyed the adventurous lifestyle of a professional sojourner, and so, every few years, she looked for a teaching position in another country. After building up experiences for a few years, she was promoted to positions of added responsibility at the schools where she taught. Eventually, she became curious about sojourning in non-Western countries. She worked in at least two non-Western countries prior to her current sojourn in

Thailand. In this sojourn, Jayna was hired as the head of the primary school.

Jayna perceived women in international schools as being pigeon-holed and limited to the primary division. In our interview she referenced several of the countries in the four continents where she had worked prior to Thailand, and concluded, "We [women school leaders] were only on the primary site." At her school in Thailand, in addition to her leadership position, Jayna was asked to teach, an added responsibility that made up approximately 20% of her overall workload. Her leadership duties were quite numerous: she hired and mentored new teachers, oversaw all the primary staff, was in charge of the special-education adjudications prior to student admittance, supported students with special needs, supervised the professional development of her staff, managed strategic planning with upper management, and much more.

During the first few months of the pandemic, she listened and responded to the many personal and professional needs of the teachers whom she supervised. She tried to include aspects of service and distributed leadership in her approach but this method clashed with the school's upper management, who used a hierarchical leadership approach. In one of their meetings, she was told, "Your style of leadership is so wrong." She told me that she felt harassed by this response, and elaborated:

> I was getting horrible emails. He [the top manager] was phoning me up, yelling at me down the phone. [...] I actually started to doubt myself, which I don't often do. [...] So I went on [an institutional website, where] they do these little courses, [and I took] a course called Leaders of Learning. And it looked at the four different types of leadership, [...and] -servant leader- came under "distributive leadership." And I realized that actually

that's where I am. I'm in the -distributed leadership- box. And I
said [to the top manager], -I'm sorry.- And he said, -Well, I
spoke to [another manager], and he […] completely agrees with
me that you are not a leader and you are not showing leadership
qualities.- He scratches [the other manager's] back, [the other
manager] scratches his back. But the problem with that [system
is that] it favors men over women, because women do tend to
distribute more. […] The other thing about [it is that] it's vulnerable to corruption. And then as soon as you stop and say, -Nope,
that's enough. I'm not okay with that,- then you're cut out of the
deal, and you're rejected.

   With close to twenty years of teaching and leading at international schools, Jayna was enthusiastic about living and working overseas,
and felt proud that her children were growing up in a cosmopolitan,
transcultural fashion. She was married to an international educator,
who likewise enjoyed the many personal and professional benefits of
the sojourning lifestyle. Jayna emphasized in our interviews how
much she loves her life. At the same time, she believed that in her
current sojourn the challenges might outweigh the benefits. She
linked some of these challenges with her difficulties in learning Thai,
saying that her children were much more fluent in Thai than she was,
and lamenting the fact that her inability to communicate not only
created social barriers outside of her work but also formed professional barriers at school, because there were many staff-members, parents,
and guardians with whom she could have only limited communication.
   Jayna also experienced numerous barriers as a leader because of
her gender. She described going to a conference in a nearby country,
at which, while the male leaders spent time socializing, the women
participants took on the lion's share of the workload. At her school,

Jayna felt that her capacity as a leader was thwarted because of her gender. She discovered that several high-level meetings had taken place without her, and that some of her decisions had been overridden by a more junior male leader.

From the outset, there was particular tension surrounding her special-education portfolio. She believed that the school was merely paying lip service in this area, and she felt uncomfortable about the fact that some of her recommendations for student advocacy had been ignored. She argued that the students in question deserved better service, and that the school's top leadership was simply not interested in engaging in conversations about this topic. These discoveries weakened her trust in the institution, and at the time of our first interview she was considering a move to another school. In our second interview, she told me that she was proceeding with this choice.

Rowan is of a similar age to Jayna and has had approximately the same amount of teaching experience. Most of her initial teaching experience took place in Canada. Then, like Jayna, she became attracted to the sojourning lifestyle, and she worked in at least three different countries before accepting her leadership position at an international school in Malaysia. This school hired her as a full-time guidance counselor, a position that came with numerous leadership responsibilities, including serving as a liaison between the students, their parents and guardian, and the upper management of the school.

Rowan came to Malaysia with prior counseling experience and was excited to live in another country. As always when sojourning, she sought intercultural learning. One way was to make friendships with local people rather than staying "bubbled" with other expatriate teachers. Her eyes twinkled when she spoke of attending a festival with one of her local friends, explaining the significance of the festival and the cultural learning that ensued. Her clear passion for intercultural learning was palpable, and it contrasted sharply with her experiences at the school where she worked. She conveyed guarded dismay about these experiences during our first interview; by the time of our second interview, the challenges had become too much for her. She had decided to leave her position at the school, and leave the country as well. At this second interview she shared her numerous professional disappointments and told the story of her "midnight run" (Stephenson, 2015) from the school and the country.

Like Jayna, Rowan clashed with the upper management of her school through her advocacy for students with known or probable special needs. She was especially concerned about some students who had what she viewed as extreme mental-health needs:

> "We have special-education students in the building but no special-education support for them. They're in our classrooms. And we're [up] against a culture that doesn't believe in special-education diagnosis. Most of them are undiagnosed, there's no documentation. We have no idea how to meet their needs, and we have no supports. It's a continual round of trying to figure out the policies and procedures [that] do not exist, and we don't even know what to do about that and where to move. Since January, I have been trying to continually have discussions with our leadership about [this]. We need these policies and procedures in place."

Rowan's calls for action to the upper management continued to be ignored, and ultimately, she came to feel that if she stayed, she would be contributing to an unacceptable neglect of the school's most vulnerable students. She concluded that the upper management was not going to listen to any of her concerns, and so she began planning for an early departure. In less than two months, Rowan was hired as a principal for another school in another country, and she felt happy that she could leave what she viewed to be an untenable condition of employment.

Discussion

The women in this study provided strong leadership within their schools on many levels, benefitting students and teachers alike. All four participants shared examples of their responsiveness to student needs, in both their pedagogy and their leadership, reflecting the prevalent view that women leaders "tend to be both more flexible and more person-oriented" (Blandford & Shaw, 2001, pp. 13-14). However, leading with emotion has often been perceived as the domain of women and has thus been devalued when compared to leading with reason, an approach traditionally associated with men. Blyth (2017, p. 6) argues that men, "in a profession that embodies the cultural expectations of women, are privileged by virtue of their gender positioning, [which] allow[s] them to more freely express their views and outlaw emotions than women."

Given what we have learned from navigating the Covid-19 pandemic in education, it seems clear that responsive leadership will be critical in ensuring that strong and relevant programming is provided in the immediate future—the type of leadership endorsed and employed by the four women in this study. The findings show that these sojourning teachers, who arrived at their schools with high energy, ideas, vision, and a willingness to take the initiative in making improvements, were quickly noticed by the schools' leaders and encouraged to harness their leadership capacities. Looking at their experiences, one might conclude that international schools, while not perfect, offer a breadth of leadership opportunities—at least for teachers early in their careers. Moreover, the professional opportunities abroad are far more numerous than in Canada, where three of these women are from, and the UK, where the fourth is from. By moving their careers to the international realm, these four women were able to accelerate the development of their educational and leadership competencies. The study shows a stark, contrast, however, between the experiences of the two women at the beginning of their careers and the two more experienced women, one working as a school principal and one on track to working as a school principal, who encountered numerous and disillusioning barriers.

The experiences of these four women are not intended to be representative of the experiences of women educators in general, nor do they necessarily represent the situations at other international schools. In small, qualitative studies such as this one, generalizability is not a goal. Nevertheless, the findings offer insights that are consistent with prior research about women in educational leadership, and highlight the need for larger studies to explore the opportunities and challenges facing women leaders in international schools.

The experiences of these women also demonstrate some barriers that require addressing, several of which are gender-specific. For instance, why is nurturing, compassionate, and distributed leadership associated with women leaders, and what messages are being delivered to children in educational systems as a result of such associations? From a career standpoint, if female international teachers experience leadership opportunities early in their careers but then discover that such opportunities stagnate as they move up, then an unhealthy and unsustainable trend of gender bias is clearly continuing in international education. An urgent challange for educational leaders is how to retain female teachers beyond lower-level leadership positions in international schools.

As far as students are concerned, the lack of special-education support experienced by the women in this study indicates that certain vulnerable students in international schools require help that is not being provided. Given that many, if not most, international schools emphasize inclusivity on their websites, such institutions must consider how to address the barriers confronting vulnerable students. The United Nations Sustainable Development Goal #4 indicates that, by 2030, high-quality education must be equitably available for all globally. This goal specifically names students with disabilities, and thus it represents another urgent leadership challenge for today's international schools.

On a broader scale, with the ongoing rapid shifts in the stakeholder bases of international education, the changing staff demographics, and the influences of large and diverse policy actors throughout the world, more leadership challenges are sure to emerge within the educational field, which will require innovation and responsiveness from the leadership teams at international schools. Women leaders will play a vital role in this response.

References

• Anzaldúa, G. (1987). *Borderlands: The New Mestiza = La Frontera*, 1st ed. Spinsters/Aunt Lute.

• Blandford, S. & Shaw, M. (2001). *Managing International Schools.* Routledge Falmer.

• Blyth, C. (2017). *International Schools, Teaching and Governance: An Autoethnography of a Teacher in Conflict.* Springer.

• Brown, C. & Lauder, H. (2011). "The Political Economy of International Schools and Social Class Formation." In R. J. Bates, ed., *Schooling Internationally: Globalization, Internationalization, and the Future for International Schools*, pp. 39-58. Routledge.

• Clandinin, D. J. (2013). Engaging in Narrative Inquiry, vol. 9. Left Coast Press.

• Dolby, N. & Rahman, A. (2008). "Research in International Education." *Review of Educational Research*, 78 (3), 676-726. www.doi.org/10.3102/0034654308320291.

• Fitzgerald, T. (2006). "Walking between Two Worlds: Indigenous Women and Educational Leadership." *Educational Management, Administration & Leadership*, 34 (2), 201-213. www.doi.org/10.1177/1741143206062494.

• Gardner-McTaggart, A. (2018). "Birds of a Feather: Senior International Baccalaureate International Schools Leadership in Service." *Journal of Research in International Education*, 17 (1), 67-83. www.doi.org/10.1177/1475240918768295.

• George, J. M. (2000). "Emotions and Leadership: The Role of Emotional Intelligence." *Human Relations* (New York), 53 (8), 1027-1055. www.doi.org/10.1177/0018726700538001.

• Harris, A. (2005). "Teacher Leadership: More Than Just a Feel-Good Factor?" *Leadership and Policy in Schools*, 4 (3), 2 01-219. www.doi.org/10.1080/15700760500244777.

• Haywood, T. (2015). "International Mindedness and Its

Enemies." In M. Hayden, J. Levy, & J. Thompson, eds., *The SAGE Handbook of Research in International Education*, 2nd ed., pp. 45-58. SAGE.

- Heater, D. (2002). *World Citizenship: Cosmopolitan Thinking and Its Opponents*. Continuum.
- Hill, I. (2015). "The History and Development of International Mindedness." In M. Hayden, J. Levy, & J. Thompson, eds., *The SAGE Handbook of Research in International Education*, 2nd ed., pp. 28-44. SAGE.
- McCaig, N. M. (2002). "Raised in the Margin of the Mosaic: Global Nomads Balance Worlds Within." *International Educator*, 2002 (Spring), 10-17.
- PIE News (May 30, 2013). "Demand for International Schools Soars in Asia, MENA." Retrieved from www.thepie news.com/news/international-school-investment-hotspots-identi fied/.
- Pollock, D. C. & Van Reken, R. E. (2009). *Third-Culture Kids: Growing Up among Worlds*. Nicholas Brealey.
- Safdar, S. & Berno, T. (2016). "Sojourners." In D. L. Sam & J. W. Berry, eds., *The Cambridge Handbook of Acculturation Psychology*, 2nd ed., pp. 173-195. Cambridge University Press.
- Sam, D. L. & Berry, J. W., eds. (2016). *The Cambridge Handbook of Acculturation Psychology*, 2nd ed. Cambridge University Press. www.doi.org/10.1017/CBO9781316219218.
- Sanderson, R. E. & Whitehead, S. (2016). "The Gendered International School: Barriers to Women Managers' *Progression*." *Education & Training* (London), 58 (3), 328-338. www.doi.org/10.1108/ET-06-2015-0045.
- Stephenson, W. T. (2015). *Midnight Running: How International Human Resource Managers Make Meaning of Expatriate Adjustment* (doctoral dissertation, University of Georgia). Athens, GA.

- Tarc, P. (2013). *International Education in Global Times: Engaging the Pedagogic.* Peter Lang.
- Ward, C., Bochner, S., & Furnham, A. (2005). *The Psychology of Culture Shock*, 2nd ed. Routledge. www. doi.org/10.4324/9780203992258.
- White, J. (2011). "'The Peaceful and Constructive Battle': UNESCO and Education for International Understanding in History and Geography, 1947-1967." *International Journal of Educational Reform*, 20 (4), 303-321.
- Whitehead, S. & Moodley, R. (1999). *Transforming Managers: Gendering Change in the Public Sector.* UCL Press.

| Chapter 08 |

My Story
to Breaking Free

Carrie Tan
Transformative Healer & Coach
Member of Parliament, Republic of Singapore
Founder, Daughters Of Tomorrow

●●●

I came and I heard

"You need to..."
"You have to..."
"You can't..."

I went along and I fumbled,

"I need to..."
"I have to..."
"I can't..."

74,268,5931 moments of doubt, confusion, judgment, frustrations, blame, self-pity, angst and giving too many f*%^s later.

I paused and I wondered.

"Maybe there is no need to?"
"Do I have to?"
"Can't I, really?"

I reached for SILENCE.
Lathered on COMPASSION.

Then I saw the shackles.
And I discovered TRUTH.

Truth is...

"There is no need to."
"I don't have to, unless I want to."
And "**I CAN.**"

The whole world may tell us otherwise.
In fact, they have told us umpteen times.
Yet, the choice is ours to find.

In SILENCE I found wisdom.
In TRUTH I found freedom.

Part 3

Forging the Allyship

| Chapter 09 |
Male Ally to Women in the Workplace,
Ally to My Wife

Shahzad Khan
Berkeley B.S.
Stanford Exec. Ed.
Global Head of Data Analytics and Strategy, Gilead Sciences

●●●

A Story of Self: The Role of Women across Cultures and Circumstance

I grew up in a household of strong women—the only boy, a middle child between two sisters and a strong mother. Although it was my father who had the high-profile diplomatic job, in our home it was clear that Mom was the boss. I fondly joke that I was raised by a pack of strong women, the proud son of a matriarch.

I was born in Pakistan, and we came over to the United States when I was a toddler. I witnessed my mother wield her loving authority not just at home but also as a diplomatic wife—a vocation that, although not paid, is certainly a full-time job. My father would often proudly say that my mother's efforts, such as leading The Pakistani Women's Association of America and hosting diplomatic soirées where she was the life of the party, were the secret to his own career advancement. He would look to her with pride as she juggled these activities along with the full responsibility of managing our home and raising three children. My sisters too are bold and empowered women, and this came about thanks to our upbringing.

As a youth, it never even crossed my mind that someone could be held back or find herself in a position of vulnerability just for being a woman. My experience was quite the opposite. I recall learning the famous nursery rhyme as a child:

"Frogs and snails,
And puppy-dogs' tails;
That's what little boys are made of.
Sugar and spice,
And all that's nice;
That's what little girls are made of."[1]

This rhyme prompted me to start crying and seek advice from my father, who calmly explained that I was rough-and-tumble and needed to take special care to look out for my mother and sisters and support them always. It's heartening to learn that our current society has also taken issue with prescriptive gender stereotypes insinuated through outdated nursery rhymes;[2] my young self was ahead of my time.

Nevertheless, I was a precocious and naughty boy. My sister, although only a year older than me, matured much faster than I did physically, emotionally, and mentally, as is often the case. The physical part proved to be an issue to my pre-adolescent self; I resorted to

---

1   www.allnurseryrhymes.com/what-are-little-boys-made-of/.
2   www.socialsci.libretexts.org/Bookshelves/Early_Childhood_Education/Book%3A_
    Child_Family_and_Community_(Laff_and_Ruiz)/04%3A_How_Does_Gender_
    Influence_Children_Families_and_Communities]_Roles_and_Gender_Stereotypes.

surprise attacks on my elder sister when I felt I had been slighted. One day I got in an especially good whack that left my poor sister sobbing. My six-year-old self was proud, but a reckoning was to come quickly. The only time my father spanked me was when he learned that I had hit my sister. I was confused about why my father was nearly crying as he disciplined me. He told me without equivocation, "Boys are never, under any circumstance, to hit a girl." At the time I thought it was unfair (she had started it, in my opinion), but the message came across loud and clear, and never again did I hit my sister.

When I was first introduced to my wife's family, who live in Romania, I was offended to learn that they had reservations about how I might treat their beloved daughter, not because of me as a person, but because of their biases and assumptions about people of Middle Eastern and Pakistani descent. As we got to know each other, however, all their misgivings were cleared up. As I've described, I was raised thinking that the whole world knew "the rules" of how to treat women, and I never imagined that there could be any issues of women being marginalized.

As I came into young adulthood, I was shocked to learn about the violence, aggression, and discrimination that women often face at home and work. During my undergraduate years at the University of California, Berkeley, I joined women's rights groups and was a self-proclaimed feminist (it's been a challenging but rewarding journey for me, and remains so to this day). To me, being a feminist means embracing the belief that women are equal to men in capability and should have equal opportunities in their careers and all endeavors. It means, moreover, that I will always do what I can to fight for such equality.

A Story of Us: Gender Inequality and What Male Allies Can Do

Even in my thirties, when I encountered my in-laws' preconceptions of me, I felt stung. But how could I blame them? Not only do women remain a marginalized population (defined as "groups and communities that experience discrimination and exclusion because of unequal power relationships across economic, political, social, and cultural dimensions"[3]), but that marginalization is more pronounced in certain cultures and groups. And there's the rub: when we lump people together, it becomes a slippery slope and a dangerous one at that—broad-stroke assumptions and stereotypes are potentially harmful on all levels. Whether it be a nursery rhyme that implies all girls are one way and all boys another, or my European in-laws arriving with preconceived notions of my character based on my heritage, this is something that we as a society must try to end. Furthermore, just as it is wrong to assume that a woman is less capable because she is a woman, so it is wrong to assume that a man is sexist or cannot learn how to be more sensitive to women's rights solely because he is a man. Such an assumption is not only wrong on an ethical level; it is detrimental to our gender-equality struggle and risks alienating and turning away potential male allies.

My country of origin, Pakistan, is the birthplace of Nobel Peace Prize laureate and women's activist Malala Yousafzai.[4] I have very fond memories of visiting the beautiful Swat Valley in Pakistan as a child[5]—the region where Malala grew up. I am proud to share a heritage with such a brave young woman. In the past few decades, Swat has fallen under the influence of more dangerous extremist

---

3   www.nccdh.ca/glossary/entry/marginalized-populations.
4   www.malala.org/malalas-story?sc=header.
5   www.en.wikipedia.org/wiki/Swat_District.

elements, and in that way, it is a different place from when I visited it as a child.

Thinking of Malala, her struggle, and her work makes me ponder several aspects of oppression against women, the nuances of women's rights, and what it means to be an ally, especially in the context of my own experiences as an American of Pakistani decent. It was an extremist Muslim faction of the Taliban that violently attacked Malala for her vocal activism for girl's education when she was only fifteen years old. In response, the majority of the Muslim clerics of Pakistan condemned the action and issued a formal Fatwa, or religious decree, against the men who attacked her.[6] Malala's father, Ziauddin Yousafzai, is an excellent example of a male ally.[7] He actively opposed the Taliban, who were trying to prohibit education for girls in the region. He also encouraged Malala to speak up for women's rights and started several schools for women's education throughout Pakistan.[8]

Regarding cultural nuances that affect women's rights, I can't help but think of head coverings. The wearing of head coverings has been perceived as oppressive to women and carries much controversy, as it has been banned in some Western countries.[9] I've had debates with my in-laws on this topic, who are in favor of these bans, whereas I am opposed to them. The women in my family who wear head coverings choose to do so out of religious belief and/or cultural preference, and they do so of their own volition, as does Malala.[10] This is my personal experience, but the lesson extends more broadly to all of us: women's rights are a complex issue, and cultural differen-

---

6   www.theguardian.com/world/2012/oct/12/malala-yousafzai-gunmen-pakistan.
7   www.en.wikipedia.org/wiki/Ziauddin_Yousafzai.
8   www.archive.org/details/iammalalastoryof0000yous.
9   www.time.com/6049226/france-hijab-ban/.
10 www.independent.co.uk/life-style/fashion/malala-yousafzai-vogue-interview-headscarf-b1858068.html.

ces nuance it further; they need to be dealt with on personal and local levels, and male allyship must be sensitive to these nuances and needs. Globalization requires broader considerations and open dialogue that acknowledges our differences, when we consider what women's rights and equality mean to us in our communities.

When discussing male allyship, I am keenly aware that I come from a position of advantage. The male ally I was in college has evolved as my understanding of women's issues, my grasp of cultural nuances, and my exposure to real challenges in society have prompted me to look deeper into myself. Most important, of course, is the direct interaction, discussion, and partnership I have experienced with women from different walks of life, who have all experienced inequality in different forms.

To sum up: the marginalization of women doesn't recognize borders; instead, it pervades society across countries and cultures. Moreover, in our struggle for gender equality, we should be careful not to cast away would-be allies due to any preconceived notions. My wife and I believe strongly that male allyship is key for accelerating women's empowerment. And, as many studies have shown, we all, as a society, tend to perform better when women are placed in leadership positions and empowered to take action.

Women Have Been Given a Raw Deal

The list of inequalities experienced by women is long and painful to read. Sexism, embedded in our societal and cultural norms, makes it hard for us to see the forest for the trees as we work for change. The rate of women in leadership is shockingly low, but the circumstances that led to this low number are not straightforward.[11] When I started

---

11 www.iwl.nichols.edu/facts-stats/

studying at one of the most progressive institutions in the world, UC Berkeley, I was amazed by all the strong women I met. Yet, when I went to my Engineering classes, I was astounded to discover a drastically low ratio of women to men—they made up no more than 30% of the students in my undergraduate courses, and this number fell to as low as 5-10% in my graduate classes.

The situation is so pernicious and insidious that we must be ever vigilant, introspective, and bold as we partner for change. Due to societal norms and institutionalized sexism, women self-censor themselves. However, research suggests that this is an area where awareness, as well as male allyship, can help.[12] Awareness of microaggressions (indirect, subtle, or unintentional discrimination against members of a marginalized group) is on the rise, and yet gender bias can be so subtle that it remains invisible.[13]

In college, I inflicted microaggressions myself, becoming part of the problem: when my Engineering, Computer Science, and Life Science friends and I met a new woman, we always assumed she was a Humanities major, reinforcing stereotypes of women not "belonging" in the hard sciences. We also tended to refer to non-STEM disciplines as "fluff" courses that wouldn't lead to meaningful work. This is terrible in itself, but underlying it was something much worse: the insidious implication that women are not capable of more challenging studies and, also, that the "fluff" courses are where they belong. On the flip side, when we encountered women in what we deemed challenging majors (the ones we were in), we would first respond with awe and then discuss how that woman was "different" for studying STEM. We thought we were being complimentary by saying a woman was "special," but our attitude implied that women on average were not equal to men and that the ones who pursued

---

12 www.thomsonreuters.com/en-us/posts/legal/women-self-censorship-penn-law/.
13 www.google.com.

male-dominated studies were the exceptions. Our comments brought undue and awkward attention to women in STEM courses that was surely uninvited and probably uncomfortable for them. Though we thought we were harmless, this was microaggression in its purest form. Knowing what I do now, I am remorseful and can't believe how oblivious I was. The most painful part is knowing that our comments must have had ill effects on the women "friends" at whom we directed these microaggressions.

This type of behavior is also common in professional life. We see fewer professional women in engineering and STEM leadership roles, a lack that reinforces these pernicious stereotypes. Women feel the bias, and it leads to fewer women wanting to be in those fields and in leadership positions. The vicious cycle will continue until we take action to end it.

As male allies, we have to work with our women partners to:

• Take broad action, including supporting more representation of women in STEM and other fields correlated to higher careers, from an early age;
• Individually and collectively look at how we use language and behavior patterns that perpetuate inequality; and
• Help to change contexts that lead to lowered expectations for young girls and women, including the expectations they have for themselves.

The idea of "death by a thousand paper cuts" has its origins in 3rd-century China, but it has taken on a new meaning in the English lexicon, describing how small acts in isolation may not be problematic, but over time can cause extreme harm.[14] This expression is often

14 www.grammarhow.com/death-by-a-thousand-paper-cuts-meaning-origin/.

used when describing the effects of microaggressions. Women face daily indignities, exclusions, and marginalization, all of forms of microaggression. A study conducted by Penn Law demonstrates how microaggressions in aggregate reinforce the "prove-it-again" expectation that women, unlike their male counterparts, must constantly prove their competence.[15] The survey provides insights into how microaggression leads to self-censorship in women[16] and reveals that:

• 58% of the women interviewed reported having been criticized for being soft-spoken or "not assertive enough";
• 54% indicated they have been hesitant to take on leadership roles because of criticism of their behavior; and
• 71% said they had been reluctant to speak up or speak frequently in meetings or group settings because of criticism of their behavior.

The study had a few positive takeaways to offer. First, male allies can partner with women to create environments that are more conducive to equal participation. Second, Gen Z are improving across all metrics related to gender-bias awareness and active allyship.[17]

For any rational human being, empirical observations coupled with overwhelming data should make it clear that gender inequality is a real and serious issue. The sheer magnitude, range, and severity of issues faced by women—including domestic violence, inequality in positions of power, lower social status, institutionalized racism, and many others—is staggering, a blight on our social well-being. I will not go into the details of these issues, as they are well covered in my wife's chapter. However, I will speak further about my personal

---

15 www.scientificamerican.com/article/microaggressions-death-a-thousand-cuts/.
16 www.law.upenn.edu/live/files/11339-wll-report-part-1-final-january-4.
17 www.thomsonreuters.com/en-us/posts/legal/male-allyship-study-penn-law/.

experiences and my perspective as ally.

First, though, let's pause to ask the critical question: what exactly is an ally?

Allyship: Constantly Evolving

The use of the term "ally" is on the rise, especially in the context of social and political movements. It is increasingly fashionable to say that one is an "ally," but what does this mean? Dictionary definitions of "ally" often fall short, and so various organizations have created working definitions. One I particularly like is from the Association for Women in Science: "Allies recognize unearned privileges in their personal lives and in the workplace. Allies act on inequalities by taking responsibility to end patterns of injustice. Allies do this through supporting others, using their position(s) of privilege to bring visibility and tangible change to the systemic issues that differentially impact individuals, groups, and communities. Effective allies recognize their own histories of oppression and use them as a tool to empathize with others without assuming shared experience or shared oppression. Being an ally is not an identity, it is a role."[18]

A Model for Analysis and Discussion

Allyship takes several forms, and different organizations have categorized allies based on different traits. While such categorizations are wide and varied, they have common themes. I find the model of researcher and educator Dr. Keith Edwards very practical; based on it, we can view allies as falling into three categories (with some overlap):[19]

---

18   www.awis.org/attention-men-ally/.

• **Allies for Self-interest.** Cis men often base their interest in gender equality on personal affiliations, such as concern for their daughters or wives. Their advocacy tends to be more personal than systemic.[20]

• **Allies for Altruism.** These allies are conscious of the injustices experienced by women but either do not realize or refuse to take responsibility for their own role in perpetuating inequality. They often view themselves as heroes of the marginalized, and yet they may become defensive when their own actions and behaviors are called out. For example, such an ally may actively work toward ameliorating the wage gap and believe he is doing a great deed, while simultaneously using derogatory language when referring to women. Seeing oneself as a hero implies superiority over others and may alienate those whom the ally purports to help.

• **Allies for Social Justice.** These allies are characterized by their focus on systems of oppression, such as institutionalized sexism. They work hand in hand with women without feeling a need to be recognized or rewarded, instead working out of genuine belief in the cause. Such allies often seek feedback and are perpetually looking to improve. They hold themselves and those around them accountable and call out harmful behavior.

While such categorizations are not perfect, they serve as a good foundation for analysis and further discussion. I find this model particularly useful because it delineates according to motivations, behavior patterns, and effectiveness.

---

19 www.keithedwards.com/wp-content/uploads/2015/05/AAID-Handouts.pdf.
20 www.dictionary.com/browse/cis-male.

Gender Inequality

What It Reveals About Our Society

When there is more equality, everyone (men included) is better off. I will jump headfirst into this section by sharing my own situation: my wife and I are both working professionals trying to balance our individual goals, dreams, aspirations, and interests with raising our family. In a world where dual income is almost a necessity for families to get by, genuine partnership is becoming ever more important. I cherish the time, consideration, and effort that my wife puts into building and nurturing our family and taking care of me, and I feel honored to do the same for her. When we share our goals and our journey as partners, we can relate to one another, provide support, and have deeper, more meaningful conversations about work, life, and the future. We value one another's perspectives, benefit from them, and work to create a future together that would be impossible if we acted in isolation. I cherish this about my marriage; I know it came with effort from both sides, and I know it is the solid foundation on top of which we can build whatever we desire.

Now let's extend this anecdote to the larger context, changing "me" to "we." Each individual is part of a larger whole, whether it be in a marriage, a family, a network of friends, a community, a corporation, a nation-state, or the world as a whole. When we work together to empower each member of our communities, the whole is strengthened even more. Of course, there are challenges to doing so. Before we jump to finding solutions, I want to highlight some systemic obstacles, knowledge of which can hopefully guide our approach. Gender inequality and its manifestations reveal much about how our societies are structured, and they also shed light on areas where we can take focused action.

Let's start with maternity leave. According to the International Labor Organization (ILO), women should be guaranteed at least 14 weeks of paid parental leave. Yet "the United States is the only wealthy country in the world without any guaranteed paid parental leave at the national level, based on data from the World Policy Analysis Center. Only a handful of other countries—all low or middle income—offer nothing."[21] In contrast, India, China, and Indonesia all offer 12 weeks of 100% paid leave, while Vietnam offers up to 4-6 months of paid leave.[22] Whilst visiting my sister in the UK, I discovered that a nurse would come two nights a week from the NHS to help my sister and her husband with their new baby, giving my sister some crucially needed sleep—a basic human need.

Next, let's consider male self-interest and the financial landscape of households. In the United States, dual-income households make up 58% of the country's total households, and this number rises to over 70% when accounting for part-time employment.[23] The number one issue that married couples fight over is money,[24] and it is also the second leading cause (behind infidelity) for divorce.[25] The studies reporting these numbers cite lack of communication between heteronormative couples, along with debt, as the most major source of stress and financial anxiety.[26] Yet marriage in the modern era is defined as a partnership; therefore, even a heteronormative male who is indifferent to injustice, a man acting out of self-interest alone, should be fighting for women's equality.

Such battles should be carried out at all levels, to the extent of your

21 www.washingtonpost.com/world/2021/11/11/global-paid-parental-leave-us/.
22 www.ilo.org/global/about-the-ilo/newsroom/news/WCMS_008009/lang--en/index
23 www.bls.gov/opub/mlr/2020/article/comparing-characteristics-and-selected-expenditures-of-dual-and-single-income-households-with-children.htm.
24 www.ramseysolutions.com/relationships/money-communication-research
25 www.ramseysolutions.com/company/newsroom/releases/money-ruining-
26 www.merriam-webster.com/dictionary/heteronormative.

sphere of power and influence. Even if you don't qualify as an ally for altruism, let alone an ally for social justice, you can, at a minimum, start as an ally of self-interest. At the simplest level, remember that an increase in your partner's income will improve your overall family situation.

Underpinnings: Larger Social Issues

As may be expected, gender inequality leads to unhappiness and depression for women.[27] What might be less expected is that it also directly leads to high depression in men.[28] Depression is a serious issue not only at the individual level but also for our society as a whole.

In a study done in the U.S., Russia, Germany, and East Asia, researchers demonstrated that cultures focused on social engagement tend to rank higher in happiness.[29] "The happiest countries are the ones who have the highest levels of a whole range of things," says John Helliwell, an editor of The World Happiness Report and a professor emeritus of the Vancouver School of Economics. "They include, especially, a willingness to trust each other to work for each other, and to come together in times of difficulty." It is fairly intuitive that income equality is highly correlated to general happiness in society.[30]

Gender inequality, by contrast, leads to stress, anxiety, depression, and despair in our homes, communities, and society. Inequalities create feelings of isolation, despair, and disruption in the cohesiveness and general health of our communities, and these in turn lead to even more social issues.

---

27   www.medicalnewstoday.com/articles/psychological-effects-of-gender-inequality.
28   www.onlinelibrary.wiley.com/doi/full/10.1111/j.1467-9566.2012.01521.x.
29   www.ncbi.nlm.nih.gov/pmc/articles/PMC4658246/.
30   www.bloomberg.com/news/articles/2015-12-21/the-relationship-between-happiness-income-inequality-and-economic

A Story of Now—Gender Equality

The Priority to Save Society, and a Case for Male Responsibility

Women's organizations at the workplace are definitely on the rise, and this is a great thing to witness. Each has a slightly different focus, but at the time of writing this chapter I have found that the vast majority of these groups are composed entirely of women—in other words, they are created by women for women. Several of these organizations started at the grassroots level and were founded so that women could come together in a safe space to share common experiences. As all organizations do, however, these groups have evolved, and now some offer more resources, such as platforms for mentorship, advocacy, and collective bargaining power.

These are heartening, valuable developments, but my wife and I still see a gap. We want to encourage more active male inclusion in efforts to improve the position of women in leadership roles, corporations, and, by extension, society.

Why the Post-Covid Era Is Critical

The fight against gender inequality has been a long and storied struggle throughout human history, replete with heroes like Susan B. Anthony, Sojourner Truth, Gloria Steinem, and Malala Yousafzai. Gains have been made, but now the Covid pandemic has set us back.[31] As of January 2021, over 2.3 million women had left the workforce in the U.S. during the pandemic, leaving only 57% of women working or looking for work—the lowest rate since 1988.[32]

At my company, we now have a hybrid work environment, in

---

31   www.unctad.org/news/covid-19-threatens-four-lost-decades-gender-equality.
32   www.cnbc.com/2021/02/08/womens-labor-force-participation-rate-hit-33.

which employees are required on site only two days a week. Firsthand discussions with mothers (and fathers) reveal that this is a very positive and welcome change. However, I have friends at other companies that require full on-site work. During the pandemic, several of these friends complained about "burn-out," and I personally know several women who have decided to leave the workforce entirely. This is a very important time for men, as allies, to work with our women partners to fight on and push gender equality forward. Hybrid work structures and lessons from the pandemic can help guide our actions.

A Clarion Call to Action for Existing and Would-be Male Allies

Becoming an ally is a journey of exploration. Although there is not an exact prescription for becoming an ally, there are several common themes to remember:

• *Educate Yourself*

Coming from a place of privilege within our societal and cultural norms, men can easily be oblivious to the issues women face. There is a lot to learn, but one key to getting started is to understand that women should not have to shoulder the burden of educating you about their history and struggle. Effort is required on your part to understand the contexts and nuances of the issues they face. Your education can take many forms, ranging from formal courses and reading to conversations with friends and joining advocacy groups. Such efforts, stemming from a sense of genuine caring, will go a long way in building trust and meaningful partnerships.

Personally, I have joined my organization's "Women at the Workplace" advocacy group and attend information series that I love and have found to be incredibly educational.

• *Listen*

Look for opportunities to learn about women's perspectives outside of your usual comfort zone, and actively listen to their experiences. Participating in women's advocacy groups that focus on systemic issues can accelerate your learning. Like everything in life, this topic is nuanced, and you should be cognizant of your role in these spaces. These forums will provide you with an opportunity to learn about why such organizations exist and the issues and solutions being addressed. Additionally, your expectations should be clear—you don't want to be "that guy" who thinks he is there to become the spokesperson for these organizations. Instead, when invited to participate in conversations, focus on trying to understand women's inequalities and struggles, and do so with empathy.

Personally, I started with the women in my life, my sisters, mother, colleagues, and friends, and—especially—my wife. I've tried to understand the issues they face and listen to how they feel about them. It was illuminating to hear my sister describe how she felt when, for a job interview, she sat in front of an all cis-male, white, and elderly panel as they spoke to her about diversity and inclusion.

• *Declare Yourself an Ally and Create Genuine, Supportive Partnerships*

This may sound simple, but a declaration is powerful. It requires tact, however, and must be heartfelt and genuine. Start by educating yourself on the issues, joining advocacy groups, and making women's issues a priority in any capacity you can. In my organization, our

CEO inspired me by example: he instituted a policy that captures the percentage of women in leadership positions and incorporates this KPI into the formula used for calculating the yearly bonus for all employees. But you don't need to be the CEO of a large organization to be an effective ally; aim to do whatever you can from your own sphere of power, influence, and context.

Male allyship entails a lifelong process of building relationships founded on trust, mutual respect, and empathy—relationships cemented through action, consistency, and accountability. Cultivating such relationships with women will allow you to gain an understanding of life experiences, identities, and perspectives that are different from your own. If you lead with empathy and understanding, you will be off to a great start, and the foundations you build will pay dividends in future inclusion and allyship.

Simple acts can go a long way. For example, women see me showing up regularly to advocacy groups, and this in itself helps to build a good foundation. When facilitating meetings, I have learned to be aware if my women colleagues are not speaking up, and in those situations, I actively ask for their perspectives (making sure, first, that they are comfortable and wish to do so). You can incorporate similar behaviors into your team's decision-making processes.

• Be Mindful of Unconscious Bias and Work Toward Growth

Men often do not take the time to think of their privilege and how it may come at the cost of marginalized groups. Research demonstrates that teaching men to be mindful of their privileges increases their sensitivity and their willingness to take action to confront sexism when they encounter it.[33] It is crucial to realize that there is not a

---

33 www.spssi.onlinelibrary.wiley.com/doi/abs/10.1111/josi.12088

finish line in this process; a growth mindset is vital.

I've been guilty in the past of acting within masculine norms and dominating team discussions. As I became more engaged in the struggle for equality, however, having honest conversations with my women partners, I grew keenly aware that I have an unconscious bias: I assume that speaking loudly and asserting my position during group meetings is necessary, and that if others are not doing the same, they probably don't have much to add. This is obviously not correct, and I have worked to educate myself and remain mindful, stepping back from those behaviors that reduce inclusiveness.

• Be Mindful of Your Communication

Be cognizant of your speech patterns and ensure that you are sensitive and intentional in what you say and how you say it. At all costs, avoid "mansplaining"[34] and break harmful social and cultural norms that are still prevalent, such as the expectations that men should speak first, speak more, or be aggressive and take control of a conversation, regardless of other people's expertise or knowledge. Another pitfall to avoid is benevolent sexism.[35] For example, in a professional setting, do not comment on women's attire, no matter how positive the comments may seem in your mind. Many men don't think of themselves as sexist, but comments that objectify women can create non-inclusive environments. True allyship means active intentionality in language and behavior that includes women as respected equals.

Finally, be humble. You will get it wrong on occasion, but be willing to take feedback, learn how your language may be harmful, and work to correct your habits. I recall being pulled aside and told by a woman colleague that I was pushing my own agenda at the cost of

34 www.merriam-webster.com/dictionary/mansplain.
35 www.wp.nyu.edu/steinhardt-appsych_opus/the-role-of-sexism-in-gender-inequality/.

hearing other people. I am so appreciative of this friend and partner; she made me look at myself and at how I can improve my communication patterns. Her advice led to my kicking some bad habits and to more productive outcomes in our team meetings.

• Model Different Behaviors

Challenge the corporate norms that have become all too commonplace, in which people are expected to be aggressive and unemotional. Instead, try to espouse behaviors and dynamics in your own workplace or sphere of influence that inspire inclusion, such as gentleness, vulnerability, empathy, and consensus-building for team decisions. As Gandhi said, "We but mirror the world," or the often quoted (though inaccurate) version, "Be the change you want to see in the world."[36] I strive to practice and improve in this regard daily. At work, my team uses consensus-building to come to group decisions, a method that is quite different from what I experienced in the past but leads to better outcomes.

Inclusive behaviors work in virtuous cycles, encouraging others to model similar behaviors. The resulting inclusive setting signals to everyone that individuals need not conform to outdated masculine norms in order to seem credible. This will also help your organization benefit from more innovation. According to a 2012 study, "female representation in top management leads to an increase of $42 million in firm value." Female leaders are particularly important for companies thriving on innovation. Notably, the more women occupying a company's C-suites and corporate boards, the better its sustainability and corporate social-responsibility initiatives.[37]

As I mentioned, my organization has taken a strong position on

---

36 www.genesisca.org/single-post/2019/06/17/be-the-change.
37 www.onlinelibrary.wiley.com/doi/abs/10.1002/smj.1955.

gender equality, and we have improved our representation of women in leadership roles by double-digit figures over the past two years. I see the effects daily in how our team meetings are conducted: we've become more collaborative, and our team's rewards and recognition, further corroborated through our performance KPIs, bear testimony to the fact that we are doing something right.

• *Speak Up, Call Out, But Also Call In*

Don't ignore acts of non-inclusion or harm, such as microaggressions. When you see such behaviors in others, take action—call them out and don't allow the actions to go unaddressed. Silence is complicity in this case, and bad behaviors need to be nipped in the bud to end the cycle. It is equally important and potentially more difficult to identify these behaviors in yourself, but it is critically important to do so by monitoring yourself and asking for critical feedback from a woman partner if you are fortunate enough to have one. Research suggests that when women believe men are acting out of belief in equality, as opposed to defunct paternalistic constructs—such as when men try to "protect" women—the men's allyship is more empowering for women and more effective.[38]

As I work to improve my own behavior patterns at work, including eliciting everyone's perspectives, I look for feedback as well as self-monitoring tools. When I see others display masculine, aggressive behaviors that may lead women partners to feel excluded, I tactfully call them out and direct the discussion back into an inclusive, consensus-building model.

---

38 www.link.springer.com/article/10.1007%2Fs11199-020-01184-4.

• *Allow Others to Step Forward*

As we work on changing societal norms, both action and inaction are important. Small acts of stepping back, like taking up less space in meetings or not jumping on a high-visibility opportunity, may allow a women partner to move forward. If you are in a leadership role, ensure that women have equal access to all opportunities or, at a minimum, that they are not bullied out of engaging by aggressive male behavior patterns. Allies in every role can look to speak less, listen more, and welcome more women's perspectives.

On my team, I am careful to ask female partners to take on responsibilities and high-visibility projects (if they desire), and I make sure that we celebrate successes as a team.

More on the Importance of Language as We Consider Male Allyship

When I learned that, in the United States, maternity leave qualifies as "disability" leave, I laughed at the absurdity of the notion, but also out of shock. In truth, it is no laughing matter. Language reveals deep truths about our values and underlying belief systems.[39] The good news is that this works in both directions; it is well established that the language we use plays a part in shaping our reality.[40]

Without getting into Whorfianism or Linguistic Relativity,[41] I advocate a practical application of Neuro Linguistic Programming (NLP) to change how we interpret reality and reframe inequalities.[42] I feel we should stop using the term "disability" when describing

---

39 www.study.com/academy/lesson/how-language-reflects-culture-affects-meaning.html.
40 www.philosophybreak.com/articles/language-shapes-reality/.
41 www.en.wikipedia.org/wiki/Linguistic_relativity.
42 www.goodtherapy.org/learn-about-therapy/types/neuro-linguistic-programming.

pregnancy, even if it just a technicality. This will not solve all our social issues, but it is surely a minor step in the right direction, and much more can be done along these lines.

Formal dictionary definitions illustrate something fascinating. "Ally" is both a noun and a verb. Merriam-Webster's first definition for the noun "ally" is "a sovereign or state associated with another by treaty or league," while its first definition of the verb "ally" is "to unite or form a connection or relation between." I like that the verb form expresses partnership. As allies to women, I believe that men should think in term of the more active, verb form of "ally," rather than the more passive, noun form.

It's heartening to see our society and language evolving in this regard: Dictionary.com designated "allyship" its 2021 Word of the Year, despite the fact that the word was just added, and other dictio-

naries have expanded their definitions of "ally."[43] Merriam-Webster itself offers this caveat in the definition of the noun form: "often now used specifically of a person who is not a member of a marginalized or mistreated group but who expresses or gives support to that group."[44]

My Personal Take: The Male Allyship Journey Continues

When I ask myself what an ally is and how I can strive to be a better ally, the answer comes down to partnership and action. Being an ally to the women in your life starts with listening, trying to understand women's perspectives, and being empathetic. I can't even imagine how enraged I would be if I heard that someone was getting paid

---

43 www.usatoday.com/story/news/nation/2021/12/06/dictionary-com-allyship.
44 www.merriam-webster.com/dictionary/ally.
45 www.forbes.com/sites/maggiegermano/2019/03/27/women-are-working-more-than-ever-but-they-still-take-on-most-household-responsibilities/?sh=7bb0403e52e9.

more to do the same job as me. Men, take a moment and think about that: you learn that you are getting paid 70 cents on the dollar compared to what your buddy gets paid for doing the exact same job. Enraged, heated? Good, now take a moment to consider that every day, the vast majority of women in the world live with this fact: they are paid less than their male counterparts. Channel the rage you would have felt if you had been dealt these cards, and then help the women in your life: your wives, your daughters, your sisters, your mothers, and your colleagues.

Being an ally is not just an activity for the workplace. You and your wife are both working long days, so why do women, by tradition, have the additional responsibilities of preparing the family meals, cleaning up, taking care of the children, and managing the household?[45] In my experience, it is best simply to jump in and start helping. Make a meal, do the dishes, start the laundry. Marriage is a partnership, and that is why I feel blessed to have the wife I do. Cooking dinner together, discussing our day, coming up with ideas (while I do the dishes), listening as she tells me about a promotion interview (while I start sorting the laundry)—these activities allow us to co-create our life and discover the full benefits of our partnership. My wife and I love discussing investments together, macroeconomics, trends in real estate, business opportunities, and career paths. We bounce ideas off each other when working on a presentation, a pitch, or, say, chapters for a book about Women in Leadership.

As my wife forges her own path, being not just a woman leader in corporate America but also a leader of women's rights, I look at her much as my father looked at my mother: with awe and admiration. She is a strong, accomplished woman and forges ahead with a positive attitude despite the system being rigged against her. She faces the daily battles that every woman faces of microaggressions and institutionalized sexism, and every day she struggles to improve the situation for herself and other women.

For my part, I try to listen more, empathize, educate myself, and get involved in my wife's groups and other groups too, through my work, our community, and our circles of friends. When I see bad behavior, I call it out. I try to be mindful of my own behavior and speech. If I catch myself acting or saying something in a manner that does not espouse allyship ideals, I seek feedback and work to correct myself, without being defensive.

I admit that I have not always been sensitive to these issues. I tend to be a jokester and have always thought of myself as a strong ally to women. My biggest offenses in the past were making light of a situation or using language that would come off as offensive to an outsider and, in hindsight, was harmful to my friends. Yes, I was an unintentional preparator. Fortunately, I have learned many lessons through discussions within formal advocacy forums and casual chat with friends, as well as countless conversations with my wife. One theme stands out: always listen, learn, and evolve. I have realized that just because my friends know I'm an ally to women and know that my habit is to be factious, this does NOT give me liberty to speak in a manner that may be harmful; such behavior is NOT okay under any circumstance. Language matters greatly. No matter the situation or context, I should speak as if I were live-streaming a public address to the world. Consistency in thought, behavior, language, and speech, regardless of context or audience—isn't this the true definition of integrity? I, like all male allies, am a work in progress, but I feel proud knowing that my male allyship will be a life-long journey.

References

Women Organizations Supporting Male Allyship – www.le-anin.org
A women's empowerment and action organization with a global reach with some great and unique angles:

- Global reach
- Starting from young girls through seasoned women professionals
- Check out their "Circles" for connecting in your own community

Association for Women in STEM - www.awis.org/
Empowering women with focus on accelerating inclusion, leadership and advancement of women in STEM

Women Entrepreneurs, WBENC - www.wbenc.org/
The largest certifier of women-owned businesses in the U.S. and a leading advocate for women entrepreneurs.

On Diversity & Inclusion, LeadingNow - leadingnow.biz/
Research Business Organization with focus on Diversity and Inclusion

Women – Men Entrepreneurial Allyship, Fairygodboss - fairygodboss.com/
Women group celebrating and encouraging women businesses that actively work with male allies

Gender Justice & Policy Transformation, Sonke Gender Justice –
genderjustice.org.za/

- South African-based non-profit organization working throgout Africa.
- Helping women and men, girls and boys can work together to resist patriarchy, advocate for gender justice and achieve gender transformation.

Additional Sources

- www.leanin.org/tips/workplace-ally
- www.wbenc.org/programs/wbenc-allyship-program/
- www.forbes.com/sites/forbescoachescouncil/2021/03/31/four-simple-but-high-impact-strategies-for-being-a-better-ally-for-women-in-the-workplace/?sh=74d56d544184
- www.hbr.org/2021/02/male-allyship-is-about-paying-attention

| Chapter 10 |

Achieving Sustainable Global Increases
in Women's Leadership Representation

Justin Hartley
Harvard MPA
Oxford MSc
Founder & CEO, Model Leadership

● ● ●

Introduction

This chapter provides a male perspective on the representation of women as leaders around the world. The opportunity to contribute, in a small way, to the discussion of such an important topic is a privilege—but it is also perhaps a risky endeavor for a man. However, as a leadership specialist, I believe that shifting a paradigm requires wide discussion of potentially contentious, sensitive, and emotive issues. Such a discussion benefits from inclusivity and participation from many groups, not solely the group in focus. After all, such inclusivity is in itself a manifestation of equality.

The chapter is arranged as follows. First, it provides a brief review of women leaders across the centuries. Second, it considers research that explores perceived differences between genders in leadership strengths and effectiveness. Third, it outlines the current trends among women filling leadership roles. Fourth, it examines various approaches, including quotas and incentivizing methods, for increasing women's presence as leaders on corporate boards. Finally, it offers suggestions for working toward the cultural and structural shifts needed to produce true equality of leadership opportunities for women and men.

Women's Leadership: A Historical Perspective

Throughout history, notable women have held senior leadership positions within different cultures all over the world. They have been responsible for some of the most important and influential leadership moments in history, however—because of cultural and societal constraints—they are leadership exceptions. Here are but a few examples:

• *In Africa*, Cleopatra VII led Egypt from 51 to 30 BC and has become one of the most famous rulers in history. During her time, she forged astute political alliances that helped Egypt to become one of the greatest powers of the age.

• *In Asia*, Wu Zetian, who ruled China from 690 to 705 AD, was a leader highly respected by both her subjects and advisers. She helped to modernize China and persuaded (whether rightly or wrongly) the majority of her citizenry to convert to Buddhism. Indian Prime Minister Indira Gandhi guided the country from 1966 to 1984 as a renowned and powerful leader. She strengthened India's national security and oversaw its launch into the nuclear age. Gandhi also helped her country to overcome chronic food shortages and increased its food security.

• *In Europe,* the heroine Joan of Arc (c. 1412-1431) helped the French army lift the siege of Orléans and led them to many more victories. Although she was burnt at the stake at only nineteen, she was later declared innocent, deemed a martyr, and eventually canonized. Empress Catherine II, who ruled from 1762 to 1796 and is more commonly known as "Catherine the Great," helped Russia to become one of Europe's great powers. In Britain, the following century witnessed Queen Victoria ruling for more than six decades (1837-1901)—one of the longest tenures of any leader in history. During this time, she oversaw rapid advancements in industry, science, politics, the military, and population growth within the larger British Empire. In the twentieth century, Margaret Thatcher became Britain's first woman Prime Minister (1979-1990) and although a polarizing figure, Thatcher is still viewed by many as one of the strongest and most talented leaders the UK has ever seen. While in Germany, Angela Merkel, whose tenure lasted from 2005 to 2021, was the first female Chancellor of Germany and is considered one of the twenty-first century's greatest leaders thus far.

• *In North America,* the African-American activist Rosa Parks came to prominence in 1955, when she refused to relinquish her bus seat to a white passenger in Montgomery, Alabama, United States. Her act of defiance became a shining beacon for the Civil Rights Movement and helped to fuel the quest for racial equality in years to come.

• *In South America,* Eva Perón displayed inspiring, influential leadership as the nation's First Lady and wife of the President Juan Perón, who led the country during his first Presidential term, from 1946 to 1952. Through the Eva Perón Foundation, she mitigated the dire plight of Argentina's poor and homeless population.

• *In Oceania*, Julia Gillard became Australia's first female Prime Minister in 2010, leading the country for three years, while in 2017 Jacinda Ardern became New Zealand's third Prime Minister and is currently still in office. Ardern is widely regarded as one of the world's greatest contemporary leaders: in 2021, *Fortune*[1] ranked her Number 1 in its annual list of the world's 50 greatest leaders.

This list of women leaders is largely political, but history has seen many influential female business leaders too, and today there are more than ever. To name just a few current women CEOs:

• Susan Wojcicki, YouTube
• Lisa Su, AMD (Advanced Micro Devices)
• Mary Barra, General Motors
• Ginni Rometty, IBM
• Maggie Timoney, Heineken USA
• Sonia Cheng, Rosewood Hotel Group
• Whitney Wolfe Herd, Bumble Inc
• Lynsi Snyder, In-N-Out Burger company
• Marillyn Hewson, Lockheed Martin

All told, the *Fortune* list included 23 women, across a multitude of professions and countries.

It is clear from this data women have a long, proven track record of effectively filling senior leadership positions. The question—and the puzzle to address is—why have societies and cultures so often witnessed so few women filling leadership roles? Even today, women's representation in leadership positions falls well below their representation within the population as a whole.

---

1   Fortune's 50 Greatest Leaders. Available at www.fortune.com/worlds-greatest-leaders/.

Perceived Leadership Strengths and Effectiveness for Each Gender

It is often argued that women's leadership styles differ from those of men. Is this true, and are women's allegedly different leadership styles viewed as more or less effective? In 2018, the Pew Research Center[2] conducted a large study on American views of leadership traits and how they intersect with gender.

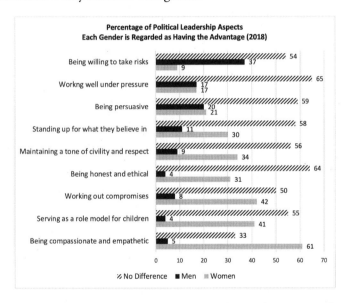

Figure 1—Percentage of **Political Leadership** Aspects Each Gender is Regarded as Having the Advantage (2018). *Source*: Original from Pew Research data (those providing no responses not shown).

---

2   This nationally representative survey of 4,587 adults was conducted online from June 19 to July 2, 2018, with support from Pivotal Ventures, using Pew Research Center's American Trends Panel. The pool was a randomly selected, probability-based sample of U.S. adults aged 18 and older. Available at www.pewresearch.org/social-trends/2018/09/20/women-and-leadership-2018/

Where political leadership is concerned (Figure 1), the survey indicated that women are regarded as being stronger than men in the areas of compassion and empathy (61% vs. 5%), serving as a role model for children (41% vs. 4%), working out compromises (42% vs. 8%), being honest and ethical (31% vs. 4%), maintaining a tone of civility and respect (34% vs. 9%), and standing up for what they believe in (30% vs. 11%). Men and women were viewed as being equally effective at working well under pressure and being persuasive. Men were seen as more willing to take risks (37% vs. 9%).

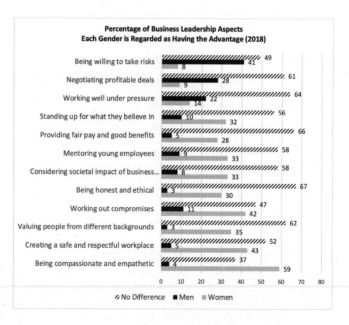

Figure 2—Percentage of **Business Leadership** Aspects Each Gender is Regarded as Having the Advantage (2018). *Source*: Original from Pew Research data. (those providing no responses not shown)

With respect to business leadership (Figure 2), women were viewed as stronger than men in compassion and empathy (59% vs. 4%), working out compromises (42% vs. 11%), being honest and ethical (30% vs. 3%), and standing up for what they believe in (32% vs. 10%). Additionally, women were perceived as being more adept than men in creating a safe and respectful workplace (43% vs. 5%), valuing people from different backgrounds (35% vs. 3%), considering the societal impact of business decisions (33% vs. 8%), mentoring young employees (33% vs. 9%), and providing fair pay and good benefits (28% vs. 5%). Men were seen as being more willing to take risks (41% vs. 8%), and more likely to negotiate profitable deals (28% vs. 9%), and work well under pressure (22% vs. 14%).

The study's list of leadership traits is by no means exhaustive and, more importantly, the study reveals only a series of self-declared views on leaders, not necessarily the traits of leaders in reality or the true attitudes of either the participants or the larger U.S. population. Its findings simply offer some insights into what Americans feel (or think they ought to feel) about gender and leadership. The important question, when we contextualize the survey in the larger discussion of gender equality, is whether the participants' self-declared views do, in fact, reflect real differences in leadership styles between men and women.

I would argue, from both my research and my personal experience, that men and women can bring different yet complementary strengths to the leadership table —strengths that, when combined, create a better-balanced form of governance than one gender alone.

When considering leadership approaches, 43% of the participants in the Pew Research Study stated that men and women were similar as leaders, while 57% said they were different. Within this 57%, 62% stated that neither approach was better, while 38% said there was a difference in effectiveness—22% believed that women were more effective, while 16% favored the men's approach.

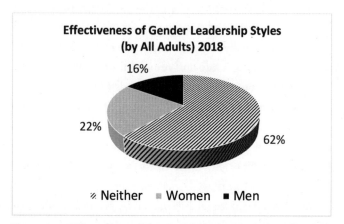

Figure 3—Effectiveness of Gender Leadership Styles by **All Adults** (2018). *Source*: Original from Pew Research data.

The next two diagrams are subsets of Figure 3 and illustrate how men and women responded as groups on this topic. Regarding the women participants in the study, 37% stated that men and women were basically similar as leaders, while 63% said they were different. Within that 63%, 62% stated that neither approach was better, while 38% believed there was a difference in effectiveness—27% believed women were more effective, while 11% favored the men's leadership style.

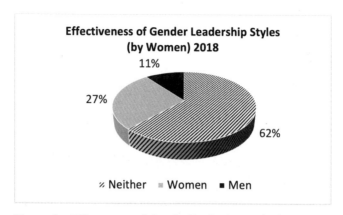

Figure 4—Effectiveness of Gender Leadership Styles by **Women** (2018). *Source*: Original from Pew Research data.

Among the men who participated, 50% stated that men and women were basically similar as leaders, while 50% said they were different. Within the 50% who considered that they were different, 62% stated that neither approach was better, while 38% believed there was a difference in effectiveness—23% believed men were more effective, while 15% favored the women's leadership style.

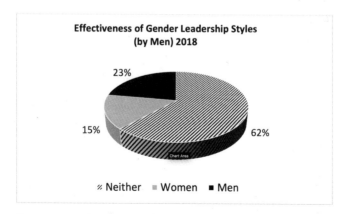

Figure 5—Effectiveness of Gender Leadership Styles by **Men** (2018). *Source*: Original from Pew Research data.

Overall, the main point to be gleaned from Figures 3-5 is that the majority of the men and women in this study claimed to view each gender's leadership styles as no more effective than the other—or, in other words, equally effective. Again, however, these results should be considered with caution, since the views come from only a very small sample of America's total population and are, moreover, self-declared, meaning that they may not represent the participants' true attitudes and behaviors in reality.

Women's Leadership Representation

For several years, the global consulting firm McKinsey has conducted research on women in the workplace. The seven editions of its findings demonstrate that women have been making some gains over time in leadership representation, though their numbers still remain well below parity with men.

The latest edition of their study, from 2021,[3] surveyed 65,000 people within the United States and Canada, working in 423 organizations, which collectively employ around 12 million people. Research from this edition (in Figure 6 below) shows that the proportional representation of women decreases as the level of seniority increases, and that, with the exception of entry-level positions, women are under-represented compared to their representation in the overall population. This gap widens the further one travels up the hierarchy of leadership.

---

3   McKinsey & Company, "Women in the Workplace 2021," September 27, 2021. Available at www.mckinsey.com/featured-insights/diversity-and-inclusion/women-in-the-workplace.

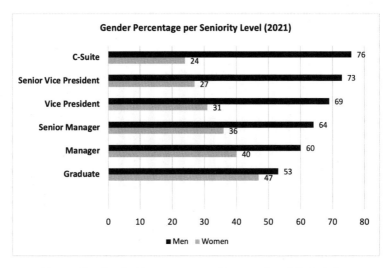

Figure 6—Gender Perecentage per Seniority Level (2021) *Source*: Original from McKinsey "Women in the Workplace 2021" data.

A review of data from the Fortune 500 Companies over the past two decades (2000-2021) shows that there has been a steady increase in the number of women CEOs in these major companies. In 2000, only two CEOs of the 500 were women; their number increased to nine in 2005, fifteen in 2010, twenty-four in 2015, and forty-one in 2021. Yet, as depicted in Figure 7 below, there has always been—and continues to be—a significant difference between the number of men and women leaders of Fortune 500 companies, with men holding the vast majority of leadership positions.

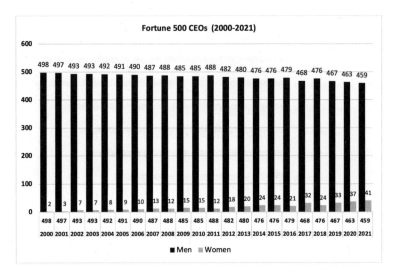

Figure 7—Fortune 500 CEOs (2020-2021). Source: Original from McKinsey "Women in the Workplace" data.

This trend of gender imbalance is also manifest in studies of women's representation on corporate boards around the world. The seventh edition of a report from the accounting firm Deloitte called "Women in the Boardroom: A Global Perspective"[4] found that, of all the corporate boards reviewed[5] only 12% of the total number of seats were held by women and an even smaller percentage of the boards, 4%, were chaired by women.

Why is women's representation in these leadership positions so low? A study from the Pew Research Center offers several possible explanations. Across both politics and business, respondents in the

---

4   Deloitte, "Women in the Boardroom: A Global Perspective," 7th edn. Available at www2.deloitte.com/content/dam/Deloitte/at/Documents/human-capital/at-women-in-the-boardroom-2022.pdf.

5   The global, regional, and country analyses are based on a data-set covering 10,493 companies in 51 countries—more than 176,340 directorships—in the Asia Pacific region,the Americas, and EMEA.

study opined that the largest barrier for women today is the need to prove themselves compared to men—a statement implying pre-existing gender biases pervading governments and corporations. Other barriers discussed were gender discrimination, women not being encouraged early enough in their careers, sexual harassment, women being held to higher standards than men, family responsibilities, and women having less interest than men in filling leadership positions. Each of these factors are major barriers for women and have historically contributed to gender discrimination and imbalances within different cultures and societies.

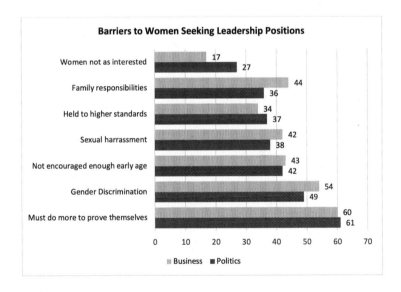

Figure 8—Barriers to Women Seeking Leadership Positions (2018). *Source*: Original from Pew Research data.

The Effectiveness of Gender Quotas as a Policy Instrument

In investigating the reasons for the gender imbalance in leadership positions around the world, and positing possible solutions for it, many researchers have studied the adoption of gender quotas, particularly as they apply to women on corporate boards. In this section I will discuss some of these researchers' findings, as well as presenting some perspectives on quotas from distinguished men and women leaders of today.

As evidenced by the international Deloitte study,[6] quotas have been increasingly applied to promote women's inclusion on corporate boards. Data from this study provides interesting insights about corporate environments in different countries and continents. In Asia, for instance, India, South Korea, and Taiwan now have quotas, while China, Hong Kong, Indonesia, Japan, Malaysia, the Philippines, Singapore, and Thailand do not. In North America, while debates on the subject are ongoing, no quotas have yet been adopted in either Canada or the United States; nor are they used in Australasia, within Australia or New Zealand. In Latin America, a few countries, such as Argentina, Chile, and Colombia, now have quotas. In Africa, Kenya employs them. Europe is the continental leader in this metric, with eighteen countries using quotas: Austria, Belgium, Denmark, Finland, France, Germany, Greece, Ireland, Italy, Luxembourg, the Netherlands, Norway, Poland, Portugal, Spain, Sweden, Switzerland, and the UK.

Many of the world's countries with no gender quotas in place have taken steps to increase women's board representation by other means. Both government and non-government bodies have shown that advocacy supporting gender diversity in corporate boardrooms does work, when combined with persistence, transparency,

---

6   www2.deloitte.com/content/dam/Deloitte/at/Documents/human-capital/at-women

and accountability.

The International Labour Organization (ILO), in their study "Women in Business and Management,"[7] notes that the UK increased its efforts to promote diversity on company boards in the early 2000s by introducing a target for the 100 largest London Stock Exchange (FTSE) companies: 25% female representation on their boards by 2015. Moreover, in 2013, legislation was enacted in the UK requiring companies to disclose the number of female and male board directors. In 2016, after the 25% target was largely achieved, the goal was reset to 33% for the FTSE's largest 350 companies. As a result, the FTSE top 100 companies' female board representation shifted from 12.5% (2011) to 32.4% (2019), while the FTSE top 350 companies' female board representation moved from 9.5% (2011) to 30.6% (2019).

In 2015, the Australian Institute of Company Directors (AICD) encouraged the largest 200 listed companies in the Australian Securities Exchange (ASX) to increase female representation on their boards from its existing 19.4% level. Voluntary measures used to promote this increase included awareness building, collaboration with supporters, and quarterly reporting requirements. In December 2019, the target of 30% female board representation was achieved in the top 100 ASX companies. In addition to these policies, the Australian Council of Superannuation Investors (ACSI), an umbrella organization representing institutional investors and international asset owners, implemented a policy to vote against companies with no female directors. Australia's Workplace Gender Equality Agency (WGEA), a government agency created by legislation, generates accessible research and data to inform the Australian community on women's participation in employment, relative opportunities, and outcomes, including pay rates for men and women.

---

7 www.ilo.org/wcmsp5/groups/public/—ed_dialogue/act_emp/documents/briefingnote

Looking at Figure 9 below, we can see which Asian countries have introduced quotas and which have not, as well as how female board representation has changed over the past seven years between 2014 to 2021. Malaysia (24%), Thailand (17.8%), the Philippines (17.7%), and Singapore (17.6%) have achieved the top four percentages of female representation on boards in the Asian region. Significantly, all of these countries do not use quotas and have outperformed those that do. Among those Asian countries with quotas—India, South Korea, and Taiwan—India and Taiwan have only slightly increased their female board representation during this period (17.1% and 7.3% respectively), while South Korea has actually decreased its percentage.

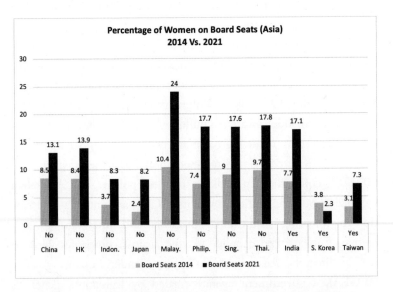

Figure 9—Percentage of Women on Board Seats (Asia) 2014 vs. 2021, By Country ("No" No Quota vs "Yes" Quota). *Source*: Original from data in Deloitte "Women in the Boardroom: a Global Perspective."

In Europe, as shown in Figure 10 below, the two countries with the highest female board representation do have quotas, these being France at 43.2% and Norway at 42.4%. Italy and Belgium, also with quotas, have made substantial gains too, with 36.6% and 34.9% respectively. However, from the combined evidence in Deloitte's study, it is clear that quotas are not the only effective approach to gender equality in the boardroom. Of the European countries that do not have quotas, several have achieved encouraging results, including Sweden at 34.7%, Finland at 32.7%, the UK at 30.1%, and Denmark at 29.6%. Their success suggests that quota and non-quota measures can be equally effective, prompting the questions which method is more preferable and does it depend upon national context?

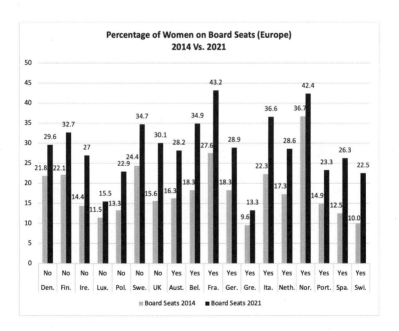

Figure 10 - Percentage of Women on Board Seats (Europe) 2014 vs. 2021, By Country ("No" No Quota vs "Yes" Quota). *Source*: Original from Deloitte "Women in the Boardroom: a Global Perspective."

Significantly, while women's board representation has been increasing around the world at encouraging rates, the number of women serving as chairs of boards does not match this change. Figure 11 illustrates that, while there has been a healthy relative improvement in the percentage of female board chairs in recent years (76.3%)—from 3.8% in 2016 to 6.7% in 2021—it remains at a very low level. When the gender split is depicted graphically—even after accounting for these increases—one can see that huge disparity remains.

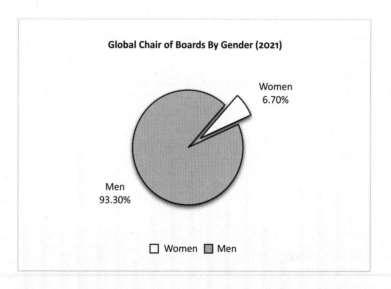

Figure 11—Global Chair of Boards By Gender (2021). *Source*: Original from data in Deloitte "Women in the Boardroom: a Global Perspective."

What does this disparity tell us? Among other things, it demonstrates that, while quotas may markedly increase the percentage of female representation on boards, their effectiveness does not spill over to chair positions. Is it feasible, then, to extend such policies and mandate that, in any given company, the board chair (just one position) must be filled by a woman? Is it acceptable to declare that being a man will automatically exclude an applicant from consideration? There is no easy answer to these questions, though it would be hard to argue that such a policy, *prima facie*, does not contain discriminatory elements.

In any case, the percentage of women on boards remains far too low, and clearly much more needs to be done. The process must begin with a more thorough understanding of why women's board representation is so disproportionately low.

Insights from Leaders of Today

The following insights will, I hope, shed further light on women's representation on boards, as well as offer a look into the future.[8] Masahiko Uotani is the President and CEO of Shiseido, a Japan-based beauty company founded in 1872. He believes that crises can provide the opportunity to re-evaluate the status quo, as when the economic bubble burst in the early 1990s in Japan. Prior to this, when things were going well, the prevalent view was "If it's not broken, don't fix it." Once the system cracked and showed vulnerability, diversity and inclusion gained traction and have accelerated in Japan ever since. Yet, despite these trends, Uotani believes gender diversity is still novel in Japan's traditional, hierarchical society. To achieve true gender parity, there must be a change in individual mindsets and, at the same time, women must develop the skills needed for professional success and must set ambitious professional goals for themselves. He highlighted softer skills, such as relationship-building, self-advocacy, and networking, as especially important. Once they develop these skills, and both genders have embraced a new mindset, he believes that women will become highly successful in

8   www2.deloitte.com/content/dam/Deloitte/at/Documents/human-capital/at-women

the boardroom.

Eileen Murray, co-CEO of Bridgewater Associates LP, is an accomplished executive with more than forty years of financial technology and corporate strategy experience. Murray's view is that, in order to make Diversity, Equality & Inclusion (DEI) a strategic priority and to create sustainable change, the results of such efforts must be measured. Organizations must keep transparent records, be held accountable for meeting their goals, and apply consistent metrics of effective leadership. In addition, she argued that investing in women at the lower management levels will increase the pool of those able to fill C-suite positions in the future. Murray pointed to the need for a company's board to have a "diversity of experience and expertise on it," so that its value can benefit the entire enterprise. She stated that, fifteen years ago, she would never have supported board quotas, but that progress toward gender parity has been, by and large, insufficient. It is reasonable to infer from these comments that Murray is now supportive of quotas in some form.

Irene Dorner, Chair of the Board of Taylor Wimpey PLC (among many other roles), has more than thirty years of banking experience, including in non-executive roles. She noted that there is cultural resistance to quotas in the UK, however the method of naming and shaming does work. She explained that she has had trouble with the idea of quotas over the years and did not want to be the token woman on the board, however she did not realize it would take decades to reach gender parity. She also pointed out that shifting the gender balance of boardrooms is easier than shifting that of whole workforces. What is needed, in her view, is DEI advocacy across organizations, with support at the executive levels reaching down through the workforce. Dorner believes such efforts must happen with regard to ethnic diversity too. She argued that setting clear targets, rather than quotas, is a better method for achieving such objectives. She stressed that women and girls need to see women—like them—in leadership positions, to build momentum. Dorner advocates the strategy of requiring half of every slate of candidates for a given position to be female, and she urged that such policies be written down in Human Resource manuals.

Executive recruiter J. Veronica Biggins has over twenty years of experience as a Senior Partner and leads the Board of Diversified Search Group. Biggins declared that boards are now looking at diversity in terms of the whole organization, yet sometimes they are more diverse than the company itself. She emphasized the importance of helping women become qualified and move up in the company in order to serve on a board. She noted that many more men than women call her seeking positions, proactively seeking to advance their career. Biggins feels that women need to be more assertive and must tell people that they're interested in serving on boards—no one will just tap them on the shoulder and offer promotion.

Quotas in Practice: Country Cases

When exploring the effectiveness of quotas, it is useful to compare their implementation in a range of different countries. Here I offer primarily European examples, as that continent has seen the most widespread and varied use of the quota system.

In 2006, Norwegian law stipulated that, within two years, women must have 40% representation on the boards of the nation's largest companies. After that two-year grace period, approximately 480 public limited companies would be subject to forced liquidation for non-compliance. The outcome of this policy was that women's board representation increased from 6% (2002) to 40% (2008). Yet, while Norway's quota certainly succeeded in increasing the percentage of women on boards, the increase, as it turned out, came largely from the same women serving on additional boards, rather than more women achieving that level of leadership. Moreover, recent studies suggest that, in order to reach the 40% quota, some companies reduced their board size rather than appointing more female directors. Studies have also shown that several Norwegian companies with a smaller pre-quota share of women on their boards de-listed from the Norwegian stock exchange between 2003 and 2009, while more Norwegian companies registered in the UK. As the UK does not have quotas, this suggests that some companies were seeking to circumvent the regulations.

In 2007, Spain became the first country in the European Union to introduce a gender quota of at least 40% on company boards by 2015. The Spanish quota extended beyond publicly listed companies, but it came without penalties. Its "soft" quota reward was to give compliant companies preference in the tendering of public contracts. Evidence is mixed on the effectiveness of this method. Observing the ten-year period from 2005 to 2014, some studies found that less than 9% of the targeted firms complied with the quota, and that these did not benefit by being awarded government contracts. The Spanish Confederation of Business Organizations (CEOE) and the Spanish Confederation of Small and Medium Enterprises (CEPYME) have both expressed strong opposition to the quota, arguing that appointments should be based on merit, capacity, and companies' competitive interests. In place of quotas, they actively promote women's career advancement by launching initiatives. Antonio Garamendi, the President of CEOE, stated, "It is always better to start from principles of voluntariness, capacity, merits, and talent, before those of obligation…and [to] increase our efforts to raise awareness in the face of discrimination."

The French Gender Quota Law, passed in 2011, requires that all listed and non-listed companies with revenues or total assets of over €50 million, or employing over 500 persons for three consecutive years, follow a stepped approach to a gender quota of 20% by 2014 and 40% by 2017. Penalties for non-compliance include treating the appointment of new directors as null and void and the non-payment of board attendance fees. This push to increase gender diversity among France's top companies has transformed its boardrooms. Prior to the quota, women represented approximately 10% of board seats. In 2018, the largest listed French companies' boards were, on average, 44% women. In the words of Douglas Branson, in his book *The Future of Tech Is Female: How to Achieve Gender Diversity* (NYU Press, 2018), "Voluntary targets didn't work [in France] … Misogyny [in business] is just like racism and sometimes this is very difficult to realize."

Italy's quota law passed in 2011, stipulating that at least 33% of any listed company's board must be female. Unlike those of other countries, the Italian law consists of a time-limited approach, earmarking a minimum of one-fifth of board seats for each gender in the first term and a minimum of one-third starting in the second term, but expiring after the third term of board appointments. Non-compliance with the quota is subject to fines ranging from €100,000 to €1 million. In 2010, women's representation on the boards of listed companies in Italy increased from 7% in 2010 to more than 33% in 2017. In December 2019, Italy announced plans to increase this threshold further, to 40%. One study, however, found that between 2013 and 2017 the number of female board seats increased by over 80% while the number of individual women on boards increased by only 51%. This suggests that, as in Norway, the same women were sitting on more boards.

In India, the Company Act (2013) imposed an "at least one" quota, requiring listed and other large public limited companies to appoint at least one woman to their boards by 2015, with fines for non-compliance. Evidence suggests that this form of quota is inadequate, however, since many companies in India have brought in only one female director to meet the minimum requirement—a "one and done" approach, rather than steadily progress toward gender equality. Furthermore, nearly 25% of these female board appointments were owners' family members.

The question arising from all of these examples is whether or not there should be a greater push for quotas, or if we should look for another effective approach that would be more sustainable in the long run. Statistically, quotas have proved to be a reliable mechanism to increase female representation on boards, especially when there are penalties in place for non-compliance. The ILO posits that quotas may also improve the allocation of talent in the labor market, helping to counteract the systemic discrimination that perpetuates the acute under-representation of women in corporate leadership positions. Quotas may also bring about positive results in the wider world by championing female role models, who can inspire and motivate more women to pursue education, professional qualifications, and careers in leadership positions.

Yet critics of gender quotas argue that they threaten meritocracy. They claim that quotas cause less qualified people to be selected for boards and deliver less efficient results than other methods. The appointees chosen as a result of quotas, these critics suggest, risk being stigmatized, and this may create a negative working environment. They argue, furthermore, that quotas may create negative influences for women in the wider world by disincentivizing the need to invest in professional and personal development. From an equity stand-point, quotas may "crowd out" other minority groups, as women are not the only group to face discrimination and inequity. Aligning with these criticisms, some of the findings from the country case studies above indicate that quotas may at times serve only as superficial, "band-aid" solutions, with companies using devious approaches to "hit the number" with the least disruption, rather than genuinely attempting to enact lasting structural change.

I believe that, in the long run, larger cultural and structural shifts must be our primary drivers for sustainable change, and that quotas, while effective in the short-to-medium term, may lead in some cases to situations that circumvent their intended purpose. Current evidence suggests that non-quota measures can significantly "shift the needle" culturally and structurally, while also producing a comparable end result to that of quotas. It appears, moreover, that a majority of men and women leaders favor these alternate approaches. Yet quotas, undeniably, lead to more female representation in leadership roles. I argue, therefore, that the most effective way forward is a concerted and coordinated promotion of non-quota measures or a hybrid approach, using quotas in the short-to-medium term while concurrently promoting non-quota measures. If quotas are chosen in the short-to-medium term, they can be phased out once initial targets are satisfied. It is my view that these approaches will effectuate deeper cultural and societal change in the long term.

I believe that we can work toward these goals by engaging in seven major initiatives:

1. Changing Mindsets: A change in mindset regarding women as leaders needs to occur in both men and women. For men, a change in mindset is required to realize and accept that women are just as capable of being leaders as men, and that there should be no difference in how they are treated. Women need to develop higher confidence in their own abilities and increase their ambition and assertiveness when seeking appointments. Increasing the public's awareness of efforts to promote gender diversity on company boards, especially within traditional hierarchical societies where diversity is still relatively new, will help enormously.

2. Increasing Accountability: Legislation, such as quarterly reporting requirements that oblige companies to disclose the number of female and male board directors, will create more transparency about gender inequities in the business world. Combined with evolving mindsets, this accountability will put pressure on companies to do better than their competitors in striving for increased women's leadership representation. Organizations should be further held accountable by the application of consistent, agreed-upon metrics that measure effective leadership.

3. Transparent, Unbiased Selection Processes: The selection processes for boards and senior leadership positions must be clearly defined, transparent, and fair. Applicants must be able to rely on the fact that the best candidates will be selected and that there will be no bias toward men or women. Stringent protocols for these selection processes will help to counteract some of the discrimination and arbitrarily higher standards that women face, and will encourage more women to aspire to and apply for such positions.

4. Ongoing Development and Training at Every Level: It can sometimes be easier to increase diversity at the board level than in an organization overall. A greater focus on developing women's leadership skills at every level, combined with an overall organizational perspective, is required. Investment in training and active support of women at the start of their careers will increase the pool of capable women who can fill leadership positions in the future. Investment throughout the organization for both men and women in the development of softer skills, such as relationship-building, self-advocacy, networking, respect, careful listening, and assertiveness, will also be beneficial.

5. Mentoring and Empowerment: Women mentors who can encourage and support the next generation of female leaders are a necessity. As the pool of trained and talented women increases in the future, more female mentors at the leadership level will be available to provide guidance and support for women at every level throughout their organizations.

6. Workplace Flexibility: Some studies indicate that women, for a variety of reasons, are more subject than men to burnout, stress, and exhaustion. In most of the world's cultures, moreover, they are still burdened with a disproportionate share of domestic and familial responsibilities, vastly increasing their stress levels. At the same time, we have seen in both the COVID pandemic and the rise of the gig economy that, as a global society, we are quite capable of operating effectively with more flexible work arrangements. Many studies have found that workers can be more productive when working from home, at least for part of the week. If more organizations offered more flexible work arrangements, women might be better able to balance their many responsibilities, both professional and domestic, and not be forced to leave their careers prematurely.

7. Governmental Policy: Governmental policy is crucial in promoting an equality of professional opportunities. Having children must be encouraged by governments without being framed as an obstruction to women's career progression, and motherhood must not be viewed as a restriction or deterrent that will prevent women from achieving their leadership potential. Just as importantly, the responsibilities of having children must be redefined as belonging equally to both parents. Many countries offer only maternity leave, not paternity leave (or else a far shorter paternity leave). In the future, parental leave should be equal for both women and men, so that families can choose when and how to have and raise their children. The option of husbands staying at home to look after the children, while their wives continue their careers, should be considered just as reasonable and natural as the reverse arrangement. Governments should also provide generous childcare support, so that single parents can continue to work and pursue their professional ambitions.

Part 4

:

The Epilogue

| Chapter 11 |

For Women Rising:
How Do We Begin?

Hungsoo S. Kim
Harvard MPA
Founding President, Center for Asia Leadership

●●●

In the early morning of April 18, I was finally able to pack my belongings in preparation for being discharged from the Seoul National University Hospital. Much earlier, in January, I had cut myself in Kuala Lumpur while cooking. I didn't know until much later how serious this incident was. Two tendons on my left hand were cut, and repairing the damage ultimately required a four-hour operation, with an additional, very painstaking six-week rehabilitation.

During this time in the hospital, I had no company with me to provide support. However, thanks to the hospital's wonderful medical personnel—fifteen altogether—I managed to survive the process. Among these fifteen personnel were twelve women, nurses to be specific, who tirelessly looked after both me and many other patients all day and all night. Though they could have fulfilled their responsibilities by rote, I could see that all the women attended to me with skill, compassion, and genuine sympathy. I know that many other patients have similarly benefited from their heartfelt care and expertise.

While on the hospital bed, though it wasn't easy, I was able to work on this publication, thanks to these women. They gave me not only expert care but a constant demonstration of the power of women's leadership. The pressure was mounting to complete the manuscript by the month's end. I had found the completion of this book extremely challenging, which perhaps testifies to my lack of knowledge and experience in the area of gender inequality. The project called for much learning, relearning, and unlearning, and now that it is over, I am thrilled to have spent time learning about such an important topic before reaching publication.

As we wrap up, I would like to offer four words that, to me, encapsulate the overall message of this book: curiosity, candor, courtesy, and courage—what I call the 4Cs. We all need these four attributes and skills to confront and overcome the challenges to gender equality that exist in our world.

Curiosity

The very first thing that the authors in this book call for is curiosity about gender inequality and what we can do to improve it. How much do we know about the sexism and gender injustice happening out there? Does it alarm us? Does it make us feel that we should take part in rectifying the wrongs and promoting good practices? What kind of conscious and unconscious biases and actions can we see in ourselves and others? How can we recognize and correct them?

Curiosity comes in two forms. Pursuing our intellectual curiosity, we can proactively take steps to learn about various contextual challenges, such as researching the history and current patterns of gender inequality and noticing comments and microaggressions that we might otherwise rush past or overlook. At the same time, pursuing our social curiosity, we can expose ourselves to new people and different perspectives, which will ultimately give us a wider range of opportunities to make a difference as leaders. Curiosity in both of these forms will serve us well throughout our lives.

In a *Harvard Business Review* article called "The Five Dimensions of Curiosity," three of these dimensions caught my interest: deprivation sensitivity, joyous exploration, and social curiosity. The first, deprivation sensitivity, is an awareness of a gap in our knowledge, which prompts us to make a relentless effort to mend it. The second, joyous exploration, involves the discovery of new fascinating aspects of our world, including the optimism associated with recognizing broader possibilities or options for solving the problems at hand. The third, social curiosity, is the keenness to understand and learn about others' needs, challenges, and hopes.

The authors in this book call for both will- and action-driven curiosity as the first steps needed to bring about positive changes, with special reference to gender equality and women's leadership.

Candor

The authors also suggest that we need to be bluntly open about the issues surrounding gender equality, such as the lack of women in positions of authority, wage gaps, patriarchy, sexism, and many more. Such candor will help all of us to speak up more freely and honestly, welcoming diverse perspectives and voices. Indeed, embracing candor and openness will allow us to hear opinions that we've never heard before, which may be starkly different from or contrary to ours. Crucially, the authors in this book advocate candor as something that

---

1   www.hbr.org/2018/09/the-five-dimensions-of-curiosity

shouldn't be just encouraged but instead expected in all of our endeavors.

Another *Harvard Business Review* article, "A Culture of Candor," argues that organizations won't be able to innovate, reinvent, respond, and function effectively if they are surrounded by too many unknowns. The more we know, the greater the chances are for our survival and growth. Therefore, "a leader's job is to create systems and norms that lead to a culture of candor." Candor, in other words, can be a game-changing element, and it ought to be taken seriously.

The contributors in this book suggest that candid leadership must begin in the areas nearest to us—at home, at school, in the workplace, in our communities, and among our friends and colleagues. If we uphold and live by a credo of candor, we will be able to make a significant difference in our societies.

Courtesy

The third C is courtesy, or respect, which the authors in this book repeatedly mention as a crucial element in achieving gender equality. This courtesy means putting ourselves in other people's shoes, not only voicing our own opinions but also listening to others in a respectful manner, especially those who have opposing viewpoints.

Gender inequality is a longstanding societal problem, and there have been countless debates and struggles in the quest to eliminate it. Often, out of fear, fatigue, or despondency, we may shy away from having important conversations on these complex issues, perhaps worrying that we might offend someone or that others will react harshly to our comments. But even if we do encounter these outcomes, we should not let our fears dissuade us, for courageous

2   www.hbr.org/2009/06/a-culture-of-candor#:~:text=Companies%20can't%20innov-ate%2C%20respond,to%20a%20culture%20of%20candor.

action is important and necessary. At times, misunderstandings will occur, but if we are genuine, courteous, and heartfelt in our intention and approach, ultimately trust will be built, and in the future more people will feel able to voice their opinions openly. We must continue to strengthen our social muscles, pursuing our curiosity with kindness and civility.

Three *Harvard Business Review* articles—"Bring Courtesy Back to the Workplace," "Do Your Employees Feel Respected?" and "Behave Yourself"—note that 20,000 employees, surveyed globally, ranked respect as the most critical leadership behavior, a uniform response among people regardless of their origins, levels of socioeconomic development, social status, and professions. Respect is clearly the key ingredient for success in any organization, as courtesy-based codes of conduct foster more effective communication, better and more trusting relationships at all levels, and the substantial reduction of workplace tension.

The authors in this book emphasize that courageous communication about difficult topics, such as gender issues, must be carried out as a duty of responsible leaders. And they unanimously agree that, as we fulfill that duty, courtesy and respect are the most effective tools for regulating the heat or tension created in the process.

Courage

The last vital element is courage. I looked up this word in the *Cambridge Dictionary*, and these definitions popped up: "to be brave and confident enough to do what you believe in," and "the ability to

---

3   www.hbr.org/2012/09/bring-courtesy-back-to-the-wor.html.
4   www.hbr.org/2018/07/do-your-employees-feel-respected.
5   www.hbr.org/2014/04/behave-yourself.
6   www.dictionary.cambridge.org/dictionary/english/courage.

control your fear in difficult situations." I also discovered that the word originates from the Latin *cor* and later the French *coeur*, or "heart." Ever since the twelfth century, "courage" has meant valor, spirit, zeal, inner strength, and bravery.

Crucially, courage requires a choice: to achieve it, you must use your own will-power, and it has to be internally maintained. For that reason, we need courage in the practice of all the elements I've discussed so far—curiosity, candor, and courtesy. We may, in principle or in our heads, agree that certain issues and challenges are important, but we also need to believe it in our hearts. When courage is combined with knowledge (head), skills (hands), and good intentions (heart), then we will be able to see its power in full force.

I learned from the several chapters in this book that courage can be exercised in two ways. One is by supporting others and helping to build up their courage, so that they can daringly face their reality and create improvements. The second is by building these "courage muscles" for ourselves. Placing ourselves simultaneously on the floor (practicing the skill of intervention) and on the balcony (practicing the skill of observation), we will be able to see when and how to take timely and effective action.

To use Mieke's and Shahzad's examples: when someone openly disrespects a woman with a sexist, condescending remark in public, you might feel nervous about calling out that behavior, for fear that you are the only person who objects to it. And in fact, you may be on your own—but if you courageously speak up, you might also discover that everybody else in the room feels the same way. Unless we voice our feelings, we won't know, and our feelings of isolation will only grow as we miss leadership opportunities. All of us will fail sometimes, but courage comes from within, and knowing this truth will help you

---

7   www.etymonline.com/word/courage.

in your next moment of decision.

When we are afraid to say something because we fear being judged, or when we make a snap judgment about others, we should also be able to call ourselves out and ask what is influencing our own judgment. All humans make snap judgments—it is part of being human—but the authors in this book advocate reflection: interrogating our own instincts and analyzing our reasons for thinking the way we do. This process can be quite revealing about our values, identities, and thought processes, and it is always beneficial to become more conscious of how we perceive and appraise a given situation. Doing so, however, requires a great deal of courage.

Gender-related challenges are often systemic in nature, and they can be overwhelming. Grappling with them requires both perseverance and decency, as well as the 4Cs. Yet, with these tools, I feel certain that we can making meaningful upward progress. The issues won't disappear or be solved overnight; instead, they are day-to-day leadership challenges that we can all participate in confronting and overcoming. Let us empower one another to gain the courage to speak candidly and to pursue our curiosity, while giving everyone respect and courtesy. This is the foundation of an inclusive community and society.

As I finish writing this Epilogue on my bed in the Seoul National University Hospital, my deepest appreciation goes to my nurses for their heart-led service. These skilled and compassionate women have tirelessly assisted me and countless others to regain their strength and gain greater hopes for living better lives. Their kindness and benevolence have enabled me to head back out into the world, and they have confirmed my belief that God created humans to work in partnerships, never alone, to live the fullness of life. Likewise, I hope all our readers have found the same inspirations, hopes and excitements from this book, believing and acting upon that our world can indeed become a better place for all of us.

I Editor's Acknowledgement I

●●●

I would like to acknowledge the help of all the people involved in the Center for Asia Leadership Initiative's noble endeavor to cultivate leaders with heads, hands, and hearts—people committed to addressing the social, business, and policy challenges that all of us face in this wonderful region of Asia—and particularly those who have had a hand in the publication of this book.

I would especially like to thank to each and every one of the authors who contributed their time, effort, and dedication to this book. In alphabetical order: Justin R. Hartley, Daria Istrate, Nikita Jain, Shahzad Khan, Mieke Klanker, Jane Jiyoung Park, Rebecca Stroud Stasel, Carrie Tan, and Ami Valdemoro. I thoroughly enjoyed our time working together over these past intense months.

Thank you also to all the additional faculty-members who took time in the past two years to share their invaluable knowledge, insights, experiences, and inspiration with a variety of communities in Asia: Rahul Daswani, Nishith Jain, Xue Jiang, Jeffrey Lamb, Richard Lum, Umar Shavurov, Dirk Soekoe, Laura Thompson, Signo Uddenberg, Junko Yoda, and Stefano Zordan.

My sincere gratitude to the supporters, co-organizers, and partners in the Center's wide array of activities, which include conferences, workshops, seminars, online learning tools, and many more. These people were instrumental in helping us run projects and organize programs successfully in a wide range of cities across Asia. These couldn't have happened without their encouragement and contributions, so I offer sincere thanks to The Asia Future Institute, The Chosun Media, The Star Media Group, Samsung Group, LG Electronics, Korean Air, Doosan, SK Group, Naver, Hyundai Motors, and the Harvard Clubs in various parts of Asia.

Among the team at CALI, I am truly overwhelmed by the support of Ursula DeYoung, for her advice in improving the quality of this volume, and of the many members of CALI Malaysia, Korea, and the

Philippines, including Luqman Hakim, Lead of Creative Design, with his ever-reliable eye for detail and good design, and Sandra Yap Program Manager and Nasya Yong Marketing & Communications Associate, who worked on the sales, marketing, and branding aspects of this book, as well as thoroughly going through the manuscript to cross-check the revisions. I also would like to thank my good buddy in all our endeavors for the Center, John Lim.

To Dr. Park Jin, Minister of Foreign Affairs of the Republic of Korea, thank you very much for taking the time to read through this volume and contribute its beautiful Foreword. I deeply respect you as a great mentor.

I offer much gratitude to the members of the Global Advisory Council: Umar Shavurov, Regional Head of CALI Central Asia; Jiro Yoshino, Head of CALI Japan; and Woosuk Choi of The Chosun Media. All of these people are great friends of CALI and have helped our efforts come to life and shine. You are wonderful sources of inspiration.

I also extend immense thanks to the fabulous medical personnel at the Seoul National University Hospital: Dr. Ji-seop Hwang, and the talented nursing team. While I was hospitalized, these great men and women made it possible for to me to wrap up this manuscript, while also conducting classes and meetings (especially for the Asian Leadership Conference 2022) over Zoom, with a space provided for me.

Finally, I would like to deeply thank my wife, Jane; and my three precious ones, Taebin, Taehee, and Lahee, for all the support you have given me, since the first volume. All of you helped this series become what it is today.

To any participants I have not mentioned by name, I sincerely thank each one of you for your assistance, generosity, and commitment, and for helping this book into print. We look forward to many more learning adventures with you!

I Contributors' Acknowledgements I

•••

Justin Hartley — I would like to dedicate this book chapter to the most incredible woman I have ever known—my Mother, Anne. Although petite in size, she was a giant in character. Mum displayed real leadership throughout her life, without holding a position of professional power or authority. She lived her values each day—and inspires me to do the same—especially those values of integrity, love, courage, honesty, trust, respect, tolerance, understanding, humility, resilience and forgiveness. Mum's legacy continues to fuel my desire to be the best person I can be and make a positive, lasting difference in the world.

Daria Istrate — Thank you to my partner, Shahzad, and to my parents, who have supported me every step of the way and who continue to encourage me to dream big. Also thank you to all the women leaders who agreed to be interviewed for this book and provided invaluable advice, anchored in their rich work and life experiences.

Nikita Jain — First of all, I would like to thank Samuel Kim, who considered my perspectives valuable on the sensitive topic of women's leadership. My chapter is a kaleidoscope of stories about my life, signifying the empowerment and support against all the odds that were given to me by my dear parents and by my sister, Manasi. Special thanks also to my husband, Siddharth, who gave me the wings I needed to be the best version of myself and to stand rock solid.Finally, a huge shout-out to all my wonderful women friends, who were my inspiration in writing my chapter.

Shahzad Khan — To my Father, who taught me many wonderful things in life including how to be an ally to women.

Mieke Klanker — I am most grateful to Jutta and Iris for laughing off some of the bizarre experiences we had together; Else for introducing me to Lean In and always being there to listen and offer me advice; Melissa and Rubiah for being inspirational and always having each other's backs;

Melissa for her openness in sharing her personal experiences and valuable guidance; Maartje for using her stage to challenge the status quo, and encouraging me to do the same; the I&D team at Deloitte, especially Mark, for persistently and steadily pushing the boundaries; the members of the Panchayat for encouraging and challenging each other to grow and thrive; and Samuel for providing me with this platform to share my perspectives. And last but not least, my family and friends for their support and advice during my ups and downs of perseveringly challenging the status quo.

Jane Jiyoung Park — I thank my God the most and would like to dedicate this work to Him, who for all these years has been my refuge and strength. Because of His unfailing love and faithfulness, here I am living a happy and purposeful life. Next, I thank my husband, for always helping me to dream of and pursue the greaterpurpose. Whenever I feel that things are overwhelming and impossible, he always cheers me up and helps me keep going. With this work, I have deeply enjoyed the thought-provoking and inspiring conversations I've had with him. My appreciation also goes to my three children, who have grown up so much now as responsible young people. I can't believe you little ones are now as tall as me; it makes me feel as if we are long-time friends. And of course, I must mention my two dads and two moms: I cannot thank you more for being my true sound-boards. Without your guidance and support, I might not be the person I am today. Last but not least, I thank my two sisters and brother-in-law: you all make me feel truly blessed because of who you are. Thank you for being part of all of my life's unfoldings. I hope we can remain this way forever.

Rebecca Stroud Stasel — This study received financial support from the Social Sciences and Humanities Research Council (SSHRC) of Canada, a support that enabled a prolonged focus and commitment to this study. Many people contributed to this study and I thank each implicitly. It took a network of people to see this project through and while names are withheld to protect the identityof the participants and the schools in which they worked, I appreciate all of the support and your recognition that research about the lived experiences of teachers and leaders in international schools is needed. I extend my deepest gratitude to the participants who gave generously of their time, insights, and energy in taking the plunge into this exploration with me. Your generosity towards your students, colleagues, and this study are inspirational. To the leaders of the schools who approved of this study to be conducted, and to the academics who supported my work both in Canada and while overseas, thank you very much. This project was dependent upon your support and for this support, I am appreciative. Organizations run far more smoothly thanks to formal and informal mentors. Thank you mentors, those of you who have supported the participants in this study, those who have supported me, and those who support leaders, teachers, and students. A special thanks to all women leaders around the world, many who navigate extra barriers to lead and whose leadership is impactful and needed. Finally, thank you family and friends for walking with me.

Carrie Tan — I would like to honor Hun Ming Kwang for being my source of inspiration and light in my spiritual journey. And all who came and went who enriched my life with material for my learning and spiritual growth.

Ami Valdemoro — To my friends at the Center for Asia Leadership, especially Samuel Kim and John Lim, thank you for inviting me to contribute this piece in service to your mission to transform leadership across Asia. I value and appreciate your dedication to ensuring that leadership in all forms is represented in your work. To my namesakes, my grandmothers Amada and Michaela, who inspired my chapter and how I show up in life, thank you for your legacy. To my mentors, particularly Cassandra Welch, Johanna Ralston, Gretchen Phillips, and Tania Longest, thank you for encouraging me to find my voice and be my own best advocate. Finally, to all of the women and men in my life who have supported me in my relentless pursuit of becoming, including my parents and my husband, Illac, my deepest gratitude.

| Center's Publications |

Rethinking Asia Series
1 - Education and Innovation
2 - Entrepreneurship and Economic Development
3 - Political and Social Change
4 - Why Asia Is Hopeful
5 - Realities & Aspirations of the New Eurasia
6 - How Leadership Can Be Taught
7 - The Future of Work: How To Prepare for It
8 - Women's Leadership Retold: What to Keep, What to Leave
   Behind, and What to Build

Asia Leadership Series
1 - Next Generation Leadership: Empowering Youth to Shape
   the Future of Asia
2 - Leadership in Development: Enhancing Your Leadership
   Effectiveness in a Changing World
3 - Leadership That Triumph: Moments of Greatness in the
   Work of Leadership
4 - Finding the Leaders in Us: New Goals for the Future
5 - Redefining Success: Learning to Lead for Change

Case Studies
Volume 1: 24 Cases